THE GRAND JUNCTION CANAL

INLAND WATERWAYS HISTORIES

Edited by Charles Hadfield

THE
GRAND JUNCTION
CANAL

by
ALAN H. FAULKNER

With 33 plates and 18 text illustrations
including maps

DAVID & CHARLES : NEWTON ABBOT

0 7153 5750 6

Set in 11 pt Garamond, 2 pt leaded
and printed in Great Britain
by Latimer Trend & Company Limited Plymouth
for David & Charles (Publishers) Limited
South Devon House   Newton Abbot   Devon

To
my wife
Anita

Contents

List of Illustrations

MAPS AND ILLUSTRATIONS IN TEXT

Preface

PROBABLY no historian can ever claim his work is complete as fresh sources of information keep coming to light and sometimes a seemingly trivial new fact can completely alter his whole previous interpretation of a situation. But there comes a stage when the facts accumulated are sufficient to produce a reasonable story and this is the case with this book.

The Grand Junction was one of the leading inland waterway companies and it has not been easy to compress the story of such an important concern into a single volume. However, every effort has been made to ensure historical accuracy, and I retain sole responsibility for this, but I would welcome hearing from anyone who can add to, or correct, my account in any way.

There is always a problem when writing about a company such as the Grand Junction, which took over two other concerns and then was taken over itself, in knowing what to include and where to stop. In this case the formation of the Grand Union Canal Company from 1 January 1929 was such a fundamental change that it makes the natural stopping place for a Grand Junction history. Similarly the detailed histories of the two Union Canals, which became part of the Grand Junction system in 1894, have been reserved for a separate work, *The Leicester Line*, already published. Indeed, it is possible that this book will be one of a series dealing with the stories of the various constituents of the present-day Grand Union Canal, which will then be completed in a book dealing with the amalgamated Grand Union itself.

A. H. F.

December 1971
  Cambridge

CHAPTER 1

The Canal is Born

IN the middle of the eighteenth century this country saw the beginning of its biggest social upheaval since the Norman Conquest, with the birth of the industrial revolution. From being basically an agricultural community the British Isles developed, in a relatively short time, into the greatest industrialised nation in the world. At the same time the agricultural revolution was transforming the countryside, with open land being enclosed into hedged fields where the proper rotation of crops could be practised. This resulted in an immense rise in productivity, which was essential to feed the rapidly increasing population, and large areas of waste and wood land were also enclosed to provide extra land for arable.

It is not generally realised to what a great extent the inland waterways of this country played a role in this tremendous development. Prior to the so-called 'Canal Age', which really started with the opening of the Duke of Bridgewater's canal in 1761, the limitations of the existing transport facilities virtually controlled the growth of many industries. Indeed without a transformation in the transport world both industrial and agricultural revolutions would have been almost impossible and certainly could not have taken place with the startling speed with which they did occur. Those centres fortunate enough to be on a navigable river could use this for the carriage of heavy goods, but further inland carts and pack horses provided the only means of transportation. The roads of the country had been neglected for centuries and were often almost impassable, particularly in winter. Although the setting up of turnpike trusts, over 2,000 of which were established by Acts of Parliament between 1700 and 1790 to maintain and improve sections of roads, considerably helped matters, their revenue, which was obtained from tolls, depended on the volume of traffic, so that less frequently used routes remained unimproved. Pack horses were less likely to delays by poor roads but were restricted in the amount they could carry, which meant their costs tended to be high.

The success of the Bridgewater Canal, built so that coal could be carried cheaply from mines at Worsley to nearby Manchester, led to the construction of a network of waterways throughout the country that revolutionised inland transport and, in so doing, helped speed on the industrial revolution with ever-increasing momentum. From the Bridgewater Canal, which by then was being extended to join the river Mersey at Runcorn, a major cross-country waterway was authorised in 1766 running to the river Trent a few miles south-east of Derby and serving the Staffordshire Potteries. This Trent & Mersey Canal was opened throughout in 1777, and running south-westwards from it at Great Haywood, not far from Stafford, the Staffordshire & Worcestershire Canal was promoted, skirting Wolverhampton and the south Staffordshire coalfield, to join the river Severn at Stourport. This route was opened in 1772. Again from the Trent & Mersey at Fradley, south-east from Great Haywood, another waterway was planned to run southwards through the Warwickshire coalfield to Coventry. Authorised in 1768, the Coventry Canal was eventually completed in 1790, parts of its line having to be built by two other companies. From the Coventry a major extension southwards was authorised in 1769 through Banbury to link up with the river Thames. At the time the Thames was navigable, albeit with difficulty, from Oxford down to London and this extension was to provide an important link with the capital. However, owing to a shortage of funds the Oxford Canal was not completed until the beginning of 1790. Meanwhile the Birmingham Canal had been promoted in 1768 to link the principal town of the Midlands with the Staffordshire & Worcestershire Canal near Wolverhampton and was completed in 1772, whilst the Birmingham & Fazeley Canal, running north-east from Birmingham to link up with the Coventry Canal near Tamworth, was opened in 1789.

One of the outcomes of the industrial revolution was the development of Birmingham into the biggest manufacturing centre in the country and it depended very heavily on the transport facilities provided by the new generation of inland waterways, both for the carriage of raw materials and the export of the finished products. Much trade was done with London and this naturally gave rise to a demand for an improved communication by water between the Black Country and the metropolis. When the Oxford Canal was at last completed in 1790 a through route did exist, but this was somewhat circuitous, involving the transit of all the Birmingham & Fazeley, most of the Coventry and the entire line of the Oxford canals and the river Thames downstream from Oxford. This route was nearly 248 miles long and included 109 locks together with numerous navigation weirs on the Thames. It is true an alternative route did exist by way of the Staffordshire & Worcestershire Canal to Stourport, the river Severn down to Framilode, the Stroudwater Canal from the Severn up to Stroud, the Thames & Severn Canal across the Cotswolds to the Thames at Lechlade, and the river down to London. Not only was this route, which was opened throughout in 1789 with the completion of the Thames & Severn, still more circuitous with 140 locks in over 280 miles, but the Thames above Oxford was in an even worse condition than further downstream, which placed a considerable handicap on traffic, whilst the numerous navigation weirs caused endless delays.

The first initiative to try and improve the inland waterways route from the Midlands to the capital came towards the end of 1791 when plans were put forward for a direct canal link from the Oxford Canal at either Braunston near Daventry in Northamptonshire, or Aynho further south in Oxfordshire, to London.[1] The need for an improved link was underlined by the great increase in trade once the through route by way of the Oxford was opened, not only with the Midlands but with the Potteries and the North

West. The principal stimulus behind the move was the extremely poor condition of the Thames navigation coupled with the roundabout route by way of Oxford. From Braunston to Brentford is 70 miles in a direct line, but 154 miles by the Oxford Canal and the Thames, whilst Aynho is nearly 55 miles from Brentford, but 120 miles by the canal and river.

Linked with the idea for a shorter canal route from Braunston to London, which soon became known as the Braunston Canal and later as the Grand Junction Canal, were other schemes to improve waterway transport. A canal from the river Soar at Leicester southwards by way of Market Harborough to the river Nene at Northampton was promoted early in 1792 and this was intended to link up with the Grand Junction by a branch, thus giving a much improved through route between London and the East Midlands. Similarly two canals were planned to improve the canal route between Birmingham and Braunston, whilst the Stratford upon Avon Canal was also promoted at this time.

The Grand Junction scheme first became public in April 1792; the *Northampton Mercury* of 14 April having a lengthy and most favourable review of the new project. The initial survey had been commissioned and paid for by the Marquis of Buckingham[2] and had been carried out at the beginning of 1792 by James Barnes of Banbury, an engineer who had previously worked on the Oxford Canal. To his great credit it seems that the Marquis was acting on the most disinterested of motives, being simply concerned to try and improve communications in the area.

Early in July 1792 notices appeared for a public meeting to be held at the Bull Inn, Stony Stratford in Buckinghamshire, at 11 am on Friday, 20 July, but on the day so many people attended that the business had to be conducted in the parish church as it was the only place large enough to accommodate them all. Barnes' survey was laid before this meeting and the plan was enthusiastically approved, it being decided to apply for an Act of Parliament as soon as possible.[3] A committee was set up to conduct the business and the subscribers were fortunate in choosing as their chairman and leader William Praed, MP, who proved a tower of strength throughout the early years of the concern. Praed was born in 1749 and followed his father into the banking profession. In 1778 he married Elizabeth Tyringham, another banker's daughter, and went to live at Tyringham Hall near Newport Pagnell. He was Member of Parliament for St Ives, Cornwall, from 1781 to 1806 when he resigned to concentrate on banking and in particular his own firm of Praed & Co, bankers of Fleet Street, which he had founded towards the end of 1801.

At the same time a select committee of five was appointed to assist the main committee, whilst Edward Oakley Gray of Buckingham and Acton Chaplin of Aylesbury were appointed solicitors and clerks to the project and Philip Box of Buckingham was appointed treasurer. A subscription list was opened and it was decided that the initial capital should be £350,000 in £100 shares, no person being allowed to subscribe for more than ten shares. An immediate call of £1 per share was made to be paid to the treasurer by 1 September to help pay for the expenses of further surveying, of the meeting and of obtaining an Act. To encourage landowners whose property would be crossed by the canal to support the scheme they were given the option to subscribe for shares in the proportion of one share for every one-eighth of a mile of their land used up to the maximum of ten shares. As an essential first step before applying for an Act Barnes was told to draw up a detailed plan and section of the proposed line and the committee was asked to approach William Jessop, one of the leading civil engineers of the day, or if he declined, some other competent engineer, to examine and verify Barnes' plans.

It was hardly to be expected that the Oxford Canal Company would look very favourably on these plans, which could mean so much of the through traffic being lost to its own canal. Its answer was to promote a canal of its own early in 1792 to bypass the river Thames and yet retain as much of the London trade on its own line as possible. This project was the London & Western, or the Hampton Gay, Canal. The route was surveyed by Samuel Simcock and Samuel Weston and was to run from Hampton Gay on the Oxford, some 6½ miles north of Oxford, to Marylebone, a distance of about 60 miles. At the same time other canals were planned to strengthen the Oxford's position; for instance a canal was to run from the Stratford upon Avon Canal at Stratford to Cropredy on the Oxford, just north of Banbury.[4] One of the first public references to the Hampton Gay scheme was in March 1792, the *Northampton Mercury* of 24 March making brief reference to the plan, whilst the issue of 14 April, in an editorial weighted heavily in support of the rival Grand Junction scheme, stressed the difficulties and hoped the Oxford would have second thoughts, particularly as it was claimed that many of its own proprietors favoured the Braunston canal.

At the beginning of September 1792 the statutory notices for the Grand Junction were published in the principal papers covering its line. These showed the main canal as running from Braunston by way of Long Buckby, Weedon, Blisworth, Cosgrove, Linford, Fenny Stratford, Linslade, Marsworth, Tring, Berkhamsted, Hemel Hempstead, Watford, Ruislip, Harrow, Southall and Hanwell to the Thames at Brentford. In addition, branch canals were included to Daventry, Stony Stratford, Uxbridge and Northampton. At the same time a second notice was issued showing a variation of the main canal south of Watford passing through Rickmansworth, Denham, Uxbridge and Harlington to Southall. The alternative scheme also included the Daventry, Stony Stratford and Northampton branches but not, of course, the Uxbridge branch.

The Grand Junction promoters were obviously in two minds about the route to be followed south of Watford. Barnes' original plan was to pass in a direct line through Harrow, whereas the alternative was somewhat roundabout as it followed the valley of the river Colne through Uxbridge. The decision to carry the main line through Uxbridge was taken at a general meeting of the proprietors on Thursday, 25 October in the County Hall at Northampton,[5] this meeting being almost certainly influenced by a resolution passed at a meeting held in Watford a few days before. This, probably organised in support of the Grand Junction project by the Earls of Clarendon and Essex, was held on 20 October and was attended by both Jessop and Barnes, who explained the merits of the two routes.[6] The meeting unanimously resolved to recommend to the Grand Junction committee that the line should pass through Rickmansworth and Uxbridge with a branch to Watford, since the line would have passed this important town some distance to the west.

At the Northampton meeting on 25 October Jessop reported that he had re-surveyed Barnes' proposed route and found it the best line possible, but he did recommend the cutting off of a bend near Leighton Buzzard and the moving of the junction with the Thames slightly downstream to where the river Brent discharged. Jessop pointed out that the main works would be at the three tunnels at Braunston, Blisworth and Langleybury, and at the Tring cutting, and that there might be problems in supplying the two summit levels with water, particularly at Tring. Jessop estimated that the cost of the main canal, which would have a top width of 42ft, a bottom width of 28ft and a depth of $4\frac{1}{2}$ft with locks $14\frac{1}{2}$ft wide and 80ft long to take Thames or Trent barges, would be £372,175, with the Daventry branch costing a further £6,000 and the Northampton branch another £18,785. By this time the subscription list totalled £361,900 and the only cloud on the horizon was the Hampton Gay proposal, but the committee was authorised to try and reach a settlement with this rival concern.

Meanwhile on 29 August at a meeting in Banbury the Oxford Canal proprietors decided to go ahead with an application to Parliament for an Act for the Hampton Gay canal[7] and the statutory notices appeared just after those for the Grand Junction in the middle of September. These showed a choice of three projects; from Shipton by way of Aylesbury, Wendover, Amersham, Uxbridge, and Harrow to Marylebone with a branch from Uxbridge to the Thames at Isleworth; from Godstow, in Oxford, to Aylesbury and then to Marsworth, where it would link up with the Grand Junction; and from Shipton to Aylesbury and

Marsworth and thereafter on a very similar course to the proposed Grand Junction line through Watford and Harrow to the Thames at Isleworth. A committee of the Hampton Gay supporters had had a meeting with some delegates from the Grand Junction and had tried to reach an agreement with them about linking up their two projects, whilst the Marquis of Buckingham had put forward the suggestion for the junction of the two lines at Marsworth, but these proposals had all been rejected by the Grand Junction. Despite a fresh approach by the Grand Junction early in November the opposition from the Hampton Gay continued unabated, and at a meeting in Woodstock on 21 November the Oxford proprietors decided by a big majority to back the Hampton Gay by every means in their power and likewise to oppose the Grand Junction.[8] On 17 January 1793 both the Oxford and the Hampton Gay proprietors petitioned the Court of Common Council at the Guildhall against the Grand Junction scheme and this petition was referred to the navigation committee.[9]

But the Grand Junction project had some very powerful backing, with many prominent landowners such as the Duke of Grafton and Earl Spencer not only supporting but in some cases actively promoting the plan and it finally triumphed over the Hampton Gay project, which was withdrawn. But this still left the Oxford in opposition and the Grand Junction eventually had to agree to a £10,000 per year guarantee of income. Negotiations also took place with the Oxford with a view to the Grand Junction leasing the northern part of its canal between Braunston and Hawkesbury. The Grand Junction was planned as a wide, or barge, canal and it was intended to widen the northern part of the Oxford to barge standards to improve access to the Warwickshire coalfields, Coventry, and it was hoped eventually further north. Although the talks failed to reach agreement this was the start of a long campaign by the Grand Junction to get other companies to widen their waterways so as to establish a barge route from London to the Midlands and the North West.

Once the Oxford had been bought off there was very little

opposition to the Act for the new canal. It had its third reading in the House of Commons at the end of March,[10] was passed by the committee of the House of Lords at the end of April[11] and received the Royal Assent on 30 April 1793. The Act[12] was law and the ambitious project was really under way. To finance the business a second call, of £2, had been made in December 1792, whilst at the end of April 1793 a further £2 call was made, with another £5 to be paid by 2 June.[13]

Under the Act the shareholders were incorporated as 'The Company of Proprietors of the Grand Junction Canal' with power to raise £500,000 in £100 shares, with a further £100,000 should it be needed. Various tonnage rates were authorised—lime and limestone could be charged ¼d per ton mile; livestock, bricks and certain other building materials, manure, pig iron, pig lead and iron stone ½d per ton mile; coal and coke ¾d per ton mile and all other goods 1d per ton mile. In addition there was a toll of ½d per ton for all goods passing between the canal and the river Thames, which had to be paid to the City of London. Fractions of a mile were charged as one mile; fractions of a ton were charged to the nearest quarter below. But various exemptions were granted. For instance the owners of wharves on the lower section of the river Brent, which was to be used for the canal, did not have to pay any tolls at all, even to the City of London, whilst troops, their horses, arms, equipment and stores were all carried toll free. Sand and gravel and other materials for making and repairing public roads, and manure for the land, could be carried free of toll provided they did not pass through any locks.

The Act provided that if the tolls to the City of London, which at the time controlled the river Thames up to Staines, did not amount to £200 from the end of April 1794 to 24 June 1795 then the deficiency had to be made up by the Grand Junction. The amount was increased by £100 each year until 1801 when the annual sum due was £1,000. This was the price enforced by the City for agreeing to the new canal joining the Thames. The agreement with the Oxford company was also written into the

Act, with special tolls being authorised on all goods passing to and from the Oxford. All coals passing from the Oxford to the Grand Junction were charged 2s 9d (14p) per ton and all other goods 4s 4d (21½p). Once the Grand Junction was opened from Braunston to Old Stratford the Grand Junction had to make good any deficiency if these tolls to the Oxford did not yield £5,000 each year, whilst once the canal was opened throughout, or after 1 January 1804, the amount was to be increased to £10,000.

Another important section of the Act concerned the appointment of Commissioners to settle all differences and assess damages and compensation payments on account of the canal works. The Commissioners, who could have no direct or indirect interest in the canal, were drawn from landowners in the five counties through which the canal passed who owned property of at least £100 in value, and certain other responsible people in those counties. In the early days of the undertaking the Commissioners had to settle a long string of disputes, but if their efforts were unsuccessful provision was made in the Act for the case to be tried by a jury. The Act contained many other clauses laying down stipulations and restrictions. Wharfage dues were set out; precise regulations governing the taking of water from streams and rivers were specified; in places the towing path had to be on the appropriate side of the canal so as not to interfere with specified property; the opening hours for the canal at various times of the year were set out; and there were rules to be obeyed by those actually navigating the canal, particularly covering the operation of the locks.

The plans deposited with Parliament in support of the Act showed that the main line was to be 90⅛ miles long with 121 locks. In addition there were to be branch canals to Daventry, Northampton, Stratford and the later addition to Watford. From the junction with the Oxford Canal at Braunston a flight of locks was to carry the waterway up to the summit level, where there was a tunnel through a ridge of hills. The descent from the summit commenced at Norton through another flight of locks and there

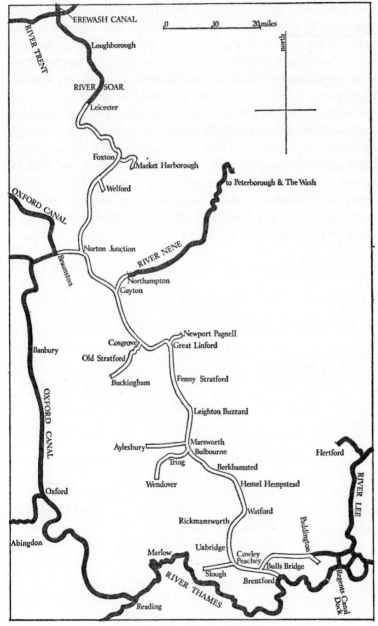

FIGURE 1. The Grand Junction Canal and its connections

was then a long level stretch to Stoke Bruerne, through a second tunnel at Blisworth. The canal then dropped down into the valley of the river Great Ouse, which was crossed near Wolverton. After climbing out of the valley there was another long level stretch to just south of Fenny Stratford, where the climb to the highest point on the canal at Tring in the Chiltern hills started. Southwards from the Tring summit the canal ran down parallel with the rivers Bulbourne, Gade and Colne through Berkhamsted, Hemel Hempstead, Watford and Uxbridge, except for a detour at Langleybury where there was to be a third tunnel. From Uxbridge there was another level stretch to Norwood and Hanwell where a flight of locks dropped the canal down to the river Brent, whose course was then followed through Brentford to the Thames.

CHAPTER 2

Building the Main Line

ONCE the Act had received the Royal Assent the company lost little time in calling the first general assembly of the proprietors at the Crown & Anchor Tavern in London's Strand on 1 June 1793. William Praed was appointed chairman and was given a

FIGURE 2. Grand Junction Canal committee seal

vote of thanks by the shareholders for his work for the canal and
a presentation of plate was made to him. Another vote of thanks
went to the Marquis of Buckingham, who had given very strong
support to the project and who was described at the meeting as
the 'Projector and Patron of the undertaking'. Indeed, the
Marquis' coat of arms was incorporated into the company's
official seal. The meeting decided that £450,000 worth of shares
should be issued, on which a call of £10 per share was ordered.
Edward Gray and Acton Chaplin were confirmed in their
appointments as clerks and Philip Box as treasurer. A committee
of thirty-one was appointed including William Praed, the Marquis
of Buckingham and such influential people as the Duke of
Grafton, the Earl of Essex, the Earl of Clarendon, Earl Spencer
and the Hon Edward Bouverie. In addition two district committees were formed; an upper to superintend the canal from
Brentford to Marsworth, and a lower the remainder of the line to
Braunston.

The main committee met two days later and James Barnes was
appointed full time engineer at a fee of two guineas per day and
half a guinea per day expenses. Barnes had to devote his whole
time to the undertaking. Another committee meeting was held
two days later on 5 June at which William Jessop was appointed
chief engineer, Edward Bouverie being asked to arrange for the
whole line of the canal to be set out so that work could get under
way.

In fact work had started on the canal at Braunston and Brentford in the early part of May and by 18 May there were already
370 men on the payroll and more hands were arriving every day.[1]
An early start was also made in the Uxbridge area, with cutting
beginning on Uxbridge Moor on 1 May.[2] Two other intermediate
points, Blisworth tunnel and Tring cutting, also saw work started
at an early date and by December 1793 3,000 men were engaged.
Most of the excavation work was done by hand but in June an
experiment was made on a section of the canal with a new
machine designed to save three-quarters of the manual labour in
cutting and removing the earth. Unfortunately, it does not appear

to have been a success so, as with most other canals being built at the time, it was the combined efforts of men and horses that dug the Grand Junction. On the administration side Thomas Homer, who had been joint clerk to the Coventry Canal, was appointed from 29 September to 'control, audit and methodise the accounts of the Company' and to superintend matters generally. Homer's salary was £500 with a further £100 per annum to procure a home, until this could be provided for him by the company. Meanwhile the company had not given up its plans to try and have a barge route to the North West and a meeting was held at Meriden in Warwickshire on 15 July with representatives of most of the companies likely to be affected attending. It was generally agreed that a wide canal would be advantageous, providing it could be done at a reasonable price, but little practical benefit came out of the conference although the Grand Junction persevered in its efforts for some time.

From the Thames at Brentford the work was making reasonable progress and the canal was opened from Brentford to Uxbridge on Monday, 3 November 1794:[3]

That part of the Grand Junction Canal from the river Thames near Brentford, to the town of Uxbridge was opened on the 3d instant for coals and all sorts of merchandise to be navigated thereon; comprizing upwards of twelve miles of this great undertaking. The opening of this part of the Canal was celebrated by a variety of mercantile persons of Brentford, Uxbridge and Rickmansworth and their vicinities, forming a large party, attended by a band of music, with flags and streamers, and several pieces of cannon, in a pleasure boat belonging to the Corporation of the City of London, preceding several barges laden with Timber, Coals and other Merchandize to Uxbridge.

Probably a fair amount of work remained to be completed, for it was not until May 1795 that toll collectors were appointed at Brentford and Uxbridge. Problems were caused at Cowley, where it was first proposed to cross the river Colne on the level, but after disputes with the millers who would be affected an aqueduct had to be built to carry the canal over the river at Cowley lock.

Similar difficulties were experienced just north of Uxbridge at Denham, where another aqueduct over the Colne had to be built at Denham lock. It is probable that the aqueduct at Cowley was not finished until the autumn of 1795, although temporary arrangements were made to pass the traffic.

There were also problems at Brentford bridge, which the company had tried to have rebuilt as it was a hazard to navigation. Jessop had carried out an inspection as early as May 1794 with a view to improving it to allow barges to pass more easily at high tide between the Thames and Brentford lock, which was then the final lock on the canal. At the time the bridge was a three-arched brick structure which needed the middle arch raising by about 3ft. Jessop proposed that a new brick structure with a 50ft span and a 28ft roadway should be built on a slightly different alignment at a cost of £2,830, which included demolishing the old bridge but did not include the purchase of buildings on the new alignment or the provision of a temporary structure. The company was unwilling to spend a large sum unless the County of Middlesex and the turnpike road trustees would make a substantial contribution and £2,500 was asked for. The county declined, as the old bridge was in good order, and the turnpike trustees declined as the county had done so. There was no alternative but to tell Jessop to make such alterations as he thought fit.

On the stretch of canal between Brentford and Uxbridge there was a major deviation from the deposited plans. From Bulls Bridge at Southall, at what is now the junction with the Paddington branch, the canal was to have run due west, passing just north of Cranford Park and Harlington village to rejoin the present line just north of West Drayton. Difficulties in obtaining the required land probably resulted in a shorter and more direct line further to the north being adopted passing through Botwell and Dawley. This deviation involved some heavy earthworks, with a long cutting at Dawley, but it saved over three-quarters of a mile of canal. Once the line was open to Uxbridge negotiations were started to establish a proper wharf there and in April 1796 an agreement was made for a short branch canal and turning basin to be built to serve wharves in the middle of the commercial part of the town.

Northwards from Rickmansworth there was another major deviation from the deposited plans. At first it was intended that the canal should run southwards from Hemel Hempstead for a long level stretch with no locks. This involved crossing the river Gade on an aqueduct and embankment near Kings Langley, a 900yd-long tunnel through some high ground at Langleybury and then a flight of locks to drop the canal down to the river Colne just north of Rickmansworth. In December 1793 a contract was awarded to Charles Jones and John Biggs for them to construct the tunnel at Langleybury, which was to be completed by 1 June 1796.[4]

Little can have been done, however, for shortly afterwards consideration was being given to the possibility of altering the line of the canal so as to avoid the tunnel altogether and in March 1794 negotiations were opened with Sir John Filmer and other landowners who would be involved. In May Barnes was told to stop all work on the tunnel and to construct a railway over the high ground at Langleybury instead, but in the following month yet another plan, this time to divert the whole line of the canal eastwards to follow the river Gade and to pass through Grove and Cassiobury parks near Watford and thus avoid the high ground, was being considered.[5] The company reckoned it could offer £12,000 to the Earls of Essex and Clarendon, who owned Cassiobury and Grove parks, as compensation for their permission for the canal to pass through and still show a saving on the costs of building the tunnel. William Praed was asked to try and reach an agreement with their lordships, but he had to report back a month later that Lord Essex had rejected the offer as inadequate. Jessop was then told to prepare a more detailed estimate of the savings to the company by avoiding the tunnel. In the autumn of 1794 the Grand Junction applied to Parliament for leave to bring in an Act to authorise the diversion, in the hope that an agreement could be reached with Lord Essex, who was still on the general committee at the time. Eventually a settlement was arrived at in November for a price of £15,000 to be paid in compensation and for the land needed, whilst in March 1795 an agreement was also reached with the Earl of Clarendon for permission to pass through Grove park with the sum of £5,000 being paid as compensation, but exclusive of the purchase price of the land.

The Act[6] authorising the diversion received the Royal Assent on 5 March 1795 and in November 1795 Barnes set out the line of the canal in Cassiobury park. In the following month the company paid a final instalment of £4,000 to complete the purchase and work started soon afterwards. It seems that the land in Grove park was never actually purchased by the company. Amongst the clauses of the Act was one authorising an additional toll of 2d per ton for all goods passing on the diverted line in view of the safer and speedier passage. Another clause insisted on by their lordships was that the canal through the two parks was to be made as ornamental as possible, hence the decorative bridge at Grove and the fine stretch of water through Cassiobury park. Work on the diverted line through the parks was completed by the autumn of 1797. The canal was extending steadily northwards and in May 1797 Barnes was told to prepare materials and carry out such parts of the work between Bulbourne, on the Tring summit, and Fenny Stratford as he thought fit.

Meanwhile in the north progress was also apparent. Work on Braunston tunnel was almost certainly one of the very first parts of the canal to be started, for early in June 1793 Barnes was told to arrange a contract with Charles Jones to drive the tunnel at a rate of £9 10s (£9.50) per yard, this price to include all the materials that would be needed. Under the contract, which Jones entered into with his partner John Biggs, the tunnel was to be finished by 1 January 1797. Progress was not meteoric and in May 1794 Jessop reported that the walls and arches had been started in two places, but he wished the contractors would get on with the work with more vigour.[7] The brickyards, which had been set up to produce the enormous number of bricks needed for the tunnel, were fairly busy but the number of imperfect bricks was high and Jessop had had to reject many of them. In addition Jessop was

Page 33
Two great Grand
Junction chairmen:
(above) William Praed,
1793–1821; (right)
Rudolph Fane de Salis,
1914–28

Page 34   Long Buckby scenes: (*above*) gauging boats at the toll office;
(*below*) during a stoppage

able to report that about two miles of canal to the east of the tunnel had been dug, whilst the deep cutting at the tunnel entrance should be finished before the end of the month. The part of the canal that had been completed was being filled with water so that boats could be used to transport bricks to bridge sites and to the locks at Long Buckby.

In February 1795 Jessop discovered that in one or two of the pits sunk by the contractors along the line of the tunnel, the lines used to ensure that the excavation underground was proceeding in the correct direction were wrong. Jessop arranged with Mr Hollingsworth, probably the company's resident engineer at the tunnel, to have them put right at once and to inspect the lines regularly in future. In June Jessop found that Hollingsworth had failed to rectify the fault, with the result that part of the tunnel had been driven in slightly the wrong direction. Jessop placed the blame principally on Biggs, whose job it was to ensure that the excavation underground followed the straight line set out by Barnes on the ground above, but Hollingsworth also came in for severe censure, his pay was cut by half a guinea a week until the error was sorted out and he narrowly escaped being sacked on the spot. As a result of this mistake Braunston tunnel has a double bend in it to this day and is thus not perfectly straight, but it is just possible to see through it from end to end despite this bend.

Apart from this mishap the work proceeded fairly smoothly, the only other trouble being that quicksands were encountered, causing the contractors difficulty. Additional shafts had to be sunk to enable the 328yd of quicksand to be worked through; this extra work cost some £4,800. The tunnel was opened on Tuesday, 21 June 1796, and at the same time the canal was opened to Weedon, some 6½ miles from the south-eastern end of the tunnel:[8]

nothing could be more gratifying than the scene which was exhibited on the opening of the Grand Junction Canal from the Oxford through Braunston Tunnel to Weedon last Tuesday. The wetness of the early part of the morning proved no obstacle to the Committee and Ladies and Gentlemen of the neighbourhood, assembled at Braunston by two o'clock when, preceded by their

C

chairman, Wm Praed, Esq, M.P., two flags and an excellent band of music, they . . . embarked on board two boats attended by an immense concourse of people . . . the Tunnel, which is 2045 yards long, is the largest and is allowed by professional men to be the best piece of work of any of the kind in the kingdom; and though so many difficulties have attended it, being through quicksands from 30 to 50 feet deep, yet it has been completed in the short space of two years—1500 yards of it having been done in the last nine months.

At this time construction of the 9 mile stretch from Weedon southwards to Blisworth, which included heavy earthworks at such places as Weedon, Heyford and Bugbrooke, was well advanced and its completion was expected early in August.[9] In fact, it was not until a month later that the stretch was completed and then there was a water shortage, which prevented the company filling it and opening it for traffic, at least for fully laden boats.[10] About the middle of September a new wharf was established at Blisworth by the firm of Roper Barnes & Co for dealing with coal, coke, salt, slates and other commodities. This wharf was to open as soon as the supply boats, that were ready loaded and waiting, could navigate down the canal.[11]

There were several deviations made from the deposited plans in this section. Originally Braunston tunnel was to be only 1,600yd long, but it was lengthened to over 2,000yd probably so as to reduce the deep cuttings at both ends. The Braunston summit was to have been over 4 miles long, but as built it was reduced to $3\frac{1}{2}$ miles. This was due to alterations at Long Buckby where ten locks were at first proposed in a close flight within five-eighths of a mile. Reduced to seven locks, the flight was spread to start half a mile further north. On the long stretch to Blisworth the plans provided for the canal taking a much more direct course. As built, however, the contour was followed on several occasions to cut down earthworks, so adding half a mile to the overall length of the canal.

There was now a $17\frac{1}{2}$ mile stretch of canal open from the Oxford at Braunston to Blisworth, but no work had been started on the stretch south from Blisworth to Fenny Stratford, apart from Blisworth tunnel, since until the tunnel was opened there was little point in proceeding further southwards and, in any case, there was no water to fill the canal. Indeed, in November 1796 Barnes had been told to concentrate on the section from Uxbridge to the Tring summit in order to get this stretch finished as quickly as possible. The canal from Uxbridge to Kings Langley was completed about the middle of September 1797,[12] whilst by the middle of November, at which time 47 miles of the main line were open and being used, Barnes reported that all the cutting had been completed from Kings Langley to Two Waters near Hemel Hempstead and all the brickwork finished except at one lock and one bridge, both of which were nearly ready.

Great delays had been caused north of Uxbridge by the nature of the ground through which the canal had to be driven—mainly sand and gravel. Water seeped in where it wasn't wanted, such as in lock excavations, and drained out where it was needed, as in the pounds. In fact pumps had to be provided at all the locks between Cowley and Cowroast on the Tring summit to keep them clear of water whilst they were being built and many had to have piles driven and sheeting put in to consolidate the loose soil on which they were built. Similarly, many miles of canal in this area had to have additional lining to make the banks completely watertight. At the time of his report Barnes expected to have the line opened to Two Waters by the beginning of December 1797.

At this time preparations had also begun on the stretch north of Two Waters; cutting was under way and was proving easier than further south and several locks were ready to be started. In addition a large quantity of timber had already been bought for this section and four million bricks were lying in strategic places along the route. The company's activities did, however, give rise to a local problem when land was required across Boxmoor Common. Although there was a clause in the company's Act which permitted trustees to sell land required for the canal, at the time the company was negotiating for a strip of land across the common there were no proper trustees in existence, the common being owned by forty joint owners who had no power to dispose of any of the land, which was preserved for the benefit of the local people. In fact the company had what amounted to compulsory purchase powers for land up to 100yd on either side of the line as shown in the deposited plans, so presumably the joint owners would feel that they must sell the land required, particularly as the canal would be to the advantage of the inhabitants of the nearby places. In 1799 at a public meeting of the people of Hemel Hempstead and Bovingdon it was decided that a committee of seven from the forty joint owners should be appointed to treat with the company. Eventually a price of £900 was agreed for the 25 acres taken for the canal and the money went to build a new wharf on the canal and a new workhouse. There must have been considerable uncertainty as to the legality of the sale of this land, for when the Boxmoor Trust was formally established by Act of Parliament in 1809 the opportunity was taken to confirm in the Act the sale of the land to the company.

In March 1798 Barnes was able to report that the canal from Two Waters across Boxmoor Common and to Berkhamsted was about three-quarters completed, and about half done from Berkhamsted to Tring. Several bridges had been finished but more delays were being caused by a shortage of bricks. These were obtained chiefly from North Hyde, near Southall, and were brought up the canal by barge. Four barges were at work, but they were not enough and efforts to get more into service had failed. Barnes was hopeful things would improve shortly as soon as men and teams of horses were released from farms where they were occupied with the spring sowing. Because of these difficulties he considered that it was hopeless to try and complete the canal to Berkhamsted by the beginning of May and to the summit by July, as had been planned at the beginning of the year, unless a very high and uneconomic rate was paid to attract men and horses so that more barges could be put into service. On the run from North Hyde three teams of horses were needed for each barge, and if eight extra barges that were needed were to be put into service another two dozen teams and the men to tend them would be required. As a result it was probably not until the autumn of 1798 that the canal was open to Berkhamsted and early in 1799 that the summit was reached.

In fact the Tring summit level itself was completed at a fairly early date. The engineers faced a formidable problem of how to carry the canal over the Chiltern hills, and eventually it was decided to drive a deep cutting through the hills near Tring. This cutting was an enormous undertaking. At its deepest point it is over 30 ft and it extends for over 1½ miles. Disposal of the excavated material presented considerable problems and much was dumped on the land on either side of the cutting, thus making it appear deeper than it really is. Apart from the sheer magnitude of the work the engineers had to contend with difficulties when both sides of the cutting started slipping, this problem being aggravated by several small springs that were discovered during the digging. The matter was finally cured by driving small tunnels, or headings, into the affected parts to drain away the water, whilst the sides of the cutting were stabilised with timber piles. The extent of this work can be gauged from the fact that it cost an extra £11,000. Work on the summit was started in the summer of 1793 at about the same time as the associated feeder branch to Wendover was begun, and both were finished by early 1797. At the time, of course, the summit was isolated from the rest of the line, but as this was a vital section which was to supply water to the canal on both sides of the summit, priority had to be given to finishing the work as quickly as possible.

Northwards from the summit there were relatively few difficulties. By November 1797 the first 2 miles through Marsworth and Cheddington, in which stretch there were nine locks, were nearly complete. Barnes explained that the reason he had started on this part of the line was because plenty of good clay was being found as the cutting proceeded, which was ideal for brickmaking. A large stock of bricks was being built up for the next summer when they could be transported by canal over the summit to where the canal was still being built, or northwards as required, with a great saving on the costs of land transport. At this time a 3 mile stretch of canal southwards from the summit was also being worked upon and on this stretch there were some ten locks and several bridges to be built.

The work proceeded uneventfully until the company started to build a bridge to carry Watling Street across the canal at Fenny Stratford. The river Ousel was not far from the canal but at a much lower level and the gradient from the old river bridge carrying the road over the Ousel to the new canal bridge would have been too steep for coaches and other horse-drawn vehicles.[13] In March 1800 the building of the canal bridge had to be deferred and Barnes was told to attend the next meeting of the turnpike trustees to try and come to some agreement with them. Finally it was decided to divert Watling Street away from the old river bridge and build a new three-arched one. In mid-June Barnes was ordered to complete the new bridge as quickly as possible, but in the meantime the canal had been opened from the summit to Fenny Stratford on Wednesday, 28 May 1800.[14] The occasion had been marked by a number of boats starting from Tring in the morning and arriving in grand procession at Fenny, with the Marquis of Buckingham and other notables attending.

Between Hemel Hempstead and Fenny Stratford there were few variations from the deposited plans except for minor differences in the siting of some locks, but in Marsworth the line was planned to pass further to the east of the village with a flight of ten locks in under half a mile carrying the canal up to the summit. As built, however, the canal passed virtually through the village and the locks were spread over a greater distance by reducing the length of the summit level. North of Fenny Stratford there were several small deviations resulting in the canal taking a more roundabout course to avoid extensive earthworks, but between Stoke Bruerne and Little Woolstone a major deviation had to be made. Originally the canal was planned to run down the valley of the river Tove in a fairly direct course, the locks being evenly spread to keep pace with the gradual drop of the river. After crossing the Great Ouse on the level a gradual climb out of the valley started through Bradwell to Little Woolstone, where there was a level stretch to Fenny Stratford. Once the decision was taken to cross the Great Ouse valley by means of an embankment and an aqueduct (see Chapter 3) the canal had to be re-routed to follow the contour and eliminate the locks, and so as to cross the Ouse slightly further upstream where the valley was steeper and narrower and hence more suitable for building an embankment.

By mid-1800 the cutting of the canal from Fenny Stratford to the Wolverton valley was well under way, Jessop reporting in April that good progress was being made and the work would be completed by the end of the year, unless there was a shortage of workmen. Meanwhile, in June 1799, Barnes had been told to start cutting the canal southwards from the bottom of the proposed flight of locks at Stoke Bruerne to the Wolverton valley, and in his report Jessop said that this work, too, was well forward and that coal should be on sale at Stratford wharf, at the end of the Old Stratford branch, in August 1800. By August the work was sufficiently far advanced for an opening date of 1 September to be forecast, most of the line already being filled with water. Flights of temporary locks had been built across the Ouse valley and a railroad was being provided across the top of Blisworth hill to link up the two ends of waterway. The railroad was completed towards the end of October 1800 and at last the Grand Junction had a through route.[15]

CHAPTER 3

Blisworth and Wolverton

ALTHOUGH the Grand Junction was opened for through traffic in the autumn of 1800 its line was punctuated firstly by the railway over Blisworth hill and secondly by the temporary canal line across the Great Ouse valley. It was to be several years before these handicaps were overcome.

From its northern summit at Braunston, on the Northamptonshire uplands, the canal had to cross the valley of the river Nene and then traverse the ridge of hills separating the Nene and the Great Ouse valleys before descending to cross the Great Ouse near Wolverton. The ridge separating the two rivers was fairly narrow and it was considered impracticable to cross it by locks, as water supplies were almost non-existent on the ridge and the summit level could only have been fed by pumping. There was thus little alternative to tunnelling and a site near Blisworth was chosen, where the ridge was at its narrowest.

From the start it was realised what a major operation the tunnel would be and early in June 1793, only a few weeks after the Act of Parliament had been obtained, Barnes was ordered to negotiate a contract with Charles Jones for making the tunnel at an all-in cost of £10 per yard. In December the contract was let to Jones and John Biggs jointly, the tunnel to be completed by 1 June 1797. Work got under way at once and in May 1794 Jessop was able to report that Biggs was getting on well with his preparatory works; he had manufactured many bricks and collected a large quantity of stone. Biggs had not started his excavations underground but was concentrating on drainage works to get rid of the water that would have made tunnelling extremely difficult.

Jessop did not speak so well of Jones,[1] who seems to have rushed into the work without making proper preparations. Working in three places Jones had completed about 24yd of tunnel, but some of the brickwork was poor and required replacing. Jones' brickworks were somewhat behind and he had no equipment ready for raising spoil from the pits. But Jessop was able to temper his criticisms with the hopeful news that following his inspection he had never come across ground more suitable for tunnelling and he considered that with good management the tunnel could be completed in much less time than had been thought likely at first.[2]

But it was not long before the contractors were running into difficulties and in September 1794 Biggs threw in his contract, saying that he was unable to complete the work on the agreed terms.[3] The company took over his equipment and materials, giving him a fair price for them and for the work he had completed, and Biggs carried on at the tunnel in the company's employment. But in May of the following year he was dismissed, along with several members of his family, after an investigation by Thomas Homer into why the expense of the completed length of the tunnel was vastly in excess of the estimate. Thereafter, responsibility for the work at Blisworth fell on Barnes, who was told to spend as much time as possible on it.[4] But despite this supervision, by the beginning of 1796 the works at Blisworth were really in trouble and almost at a standstill, with an uncontrollable amount of water drowning out tunnelling operations. Jessop seems to have lost heart at this, for he wrote to Praed recommending that the tunnel be abandoned altogether and the canal carried over Blisworth hill by locks so as not to delay the completion of the through route. Both Jessop and Barnes were asked to investigate the troubles at Blisworth and Jessop was asked for more details of his lock plan.

Both reports were ready early in February 1796; whilst Jessop was all for forgetting the tunnel, Barnes considered a tunnel not only feasible but much more satisfactory, although he favoured a slightly different course. Before a decision was taken, outside help was sought in the shape of John Rennie and Robert Whitworth, both of whom were asked to examine the works at Blisworth and report on the locks proposal. Their report was delivered by the middle of May and it recommended the building of the tunnel, but on a slightly different line starting just to the east of the original line at the north end, crossing, and then finishing about 130yd west of the original line at the south end. Barnes, vindicated, then offered to complete the tunnel by June 1799 at a price of not more than £16 per yard for the 3,000yd long tunnel, and under a £5,000 penalty, providing the company would finance him. This offer was accepted and in June 1796 Barnes was put in sole charge of the works at Blisworth.[5] In September he was allowed to proceed with the tunnelling and with the deep cuttings at both ends, but was told to limit his expenses to no more than £7,000 before 1 May 1797.

Work on the new alignment proceeded slowly, but in March 1797 it was decided that in an effort to try and speed things up elsewhere on the line work on the tunnel should be discontinued, Barnes being told to carry out such works only as would be necessary to preserve what had already been carried out. But Barnes pleaded to be allowed to keep working on the heading, the small pilot tunnel cut underneath the main tunnel to act as a drain to take off the unwanted water in the hill. Barnes was fully aware that the first attempt had failed because of the lack of such a precaution, and he realised that the completion of the main tunnel must be entirely dependent on the heading being completed. Fortunately his pleas were heeded, but only a skeleton staff of about six men was kept at Blisworth for this purpose. At the southern end of the tunnel in Stoke Bruerne the heading extended some way beyond the end of the workings to where the land fell and the water could drain away naturally.

Meanwhile, as early as November 1796 Barnes had been told to plan a road over the top of Blisworth hill, following the course of the intended tunnel, and in August 1797 it was decided to spend £250 on making it, to run from Pickford's wharf in Blisworth across the Northampton to Towcester turnpike and then over the hill to join the Northampton to Old Stratford turnpike, a total distance of some 3½ miles. Tolls were fixed for the use of the road, which did not take long to build, and it was soon of some importance to the company in that it created an outlet for the canal from its temporary terminus at Blisworth. Already many boats were trading to the village, where extensive wharves and warehouses had been set up, two new inns established by the canal, several thousand tons of coal were in store and a boatyard had been founded where new craft were being built.[6]

In November 1797 Barnes was able to report that work on the heading was getting on well, and that the amount of water encountered was so great that it would have been quite impossible to drive the main tunnel without the heading. Once completed, however, Barnes was confident excavation of the tunnel could take place along its whole length simultaneously.

By 1798, when work on other parts of the canal was proceeding well, the company began to realise that the task at Blisworth was as far from completion as ever and the withdrawal of the main labour force had been a short-sighted move. In August there was a proposal that Benjamin Outram, the tramroad engineer, should be called in to view the whole length of the canal, but the idea was turned down. It is probable that the toll road over the hill was not entirely satisfactory, particularly for the heavier type of goods, for in March 1799 Jessop proposed that a cast iron railway should be built over the top of the hill from Blisworth to Cosgrove. He was then asked to make a survey with Barnes. Both engineers had submitted their reports by the following month and after a general meeting of the company in June the go-ahead was given. The original intention was for the railway to continue through Stoke Bruerne to Old Stratford, following the course of the turnpike road. At Old Stratford a connection with the southern part of the canal would have been made by means of the Old Stratford branch from Cosgrove, but in June 1799 Barnes was ordered to start work on the canal from Stoke Bruerne southwards to Cosgrove and Old Stratford, as it was realised that it would be far better to keep the railway as short as possible.

In July a small sub-committee was set up under William Praed to plan the railway scheme or to find a more suitable way of conveying goods over the hill whilst the tunnel was under construction. The sub-committee, accompanied by Jessop and Barnes, attended a series of tests carried out on a colliery railway at Measham owned by Joseph Wilkes. Wilkes was a member of the Grand Junction committee and a leading supporter of the railway proposal. The sub-committee must have been impressed with what they saw for, after hearing from Jessop that he thought the tunnel would take from two to three years to complete, the railway plan for Blisworth was adopted. But an immediate problem arose in that Jessop and Barnes, when planning the line of the railway, wanted to deviate more than 100yd from the Parliamentary line in places to ease some of the gradients. The permission of the Duke of Grafton, the local landowner, was essential before a start could be made and Praed was deputed to contact him. But the Duke was not inclined to be at all helpful to the company. Not only was he disappointed that the work on the tunnel was being deferred, but he was concerned as to how some of his tenants would be affected by the railway, and he also wanted precautions taken to prevent those employed on it from becoming a nuisance in the neighbouring villages. Praed tried to reassure the Duke, but his lordship was still far from happy, although he grudgingly told Praed he would consider more detailed proposals. But the company, obviously afraid of protracted negotiations holding up the project, decided early in October to amend the line of the railway so as to follow the course of the canal as set out in the Act. Both Barnes and Outram, who had now been called in, had studied the amended line and both considered it perfectly practicable; although some of the gradients would be steeper, the overall length of the line would be shorter.

Outram then produced his specification for the railway. Eight yards of properly drained land would be needed for the width of the line, of which the centre 6yd would be covered with stones or other hard materials to a depth of 12in. Stone block sleepers, obtainable from local quarries, were to be used in which two holes were to be drilled and plugged with wood. The rails were to be cast iron, each one being 1yd long, weighing 37lb and being fastened to the sleepers by large nails driven into the wooden plugs. Outram envisaged that the waggons would carry from 1½ to 2 tons. His estimate for the double track railway was £9,750, of which £6,604 was for the 4,600yd stretch from Blisworth to Stoke Bruerne, £1,921 for the 1,400yd extension from Stoke Bruerne to just south of the Old Stratford turnpike where the canal was being built, and £1,225 for 80 waggons, 4 cranes and other incidentals. Of the £8,525 for the actual railway works, by far the largest item was for 405 tons of cast iron rails costing £5,470. The stone blocks, with the oak plugs and iron spikes, cost £910, the earthworks £665, forming the roadbed £840 and drainage and other works £640. Outram's estimate was accepted by the company, a formal contract being drawn up with a clause whereby Outram was to guarantee the line for three years from its completion. He started on the work straightaway and completed the railway, not without a show of impatience by the company since it was supposed to have been finished by 1 August, in October 1800.

Early in 1801, following a series of visits to railways in Derbyshire by two of the company's officers, a set of regulations was issued governing its day to day use, since some form of control was found to be essential. In May a short extension of about 100yd was authorised at the north end of the line to take it from the public wharf in Blisworth across the Towcester turnpike to Pickford's wharf. All manner of goods were carried on the line and Blisworth and Stoke Bruerne must have taken on the appearance of small ports. Coal, pig iron, stone, slate, bricks, timber, lime, manufactured goods and agricultural products were all carried as through trade on the canal at this time and thus presumably on the railway as well.[7] Carriage of the goods was entirely in the hands of private contractors, the company being unwilling to get involved. The rails used for the line were 'L' shaped and were fixed to the sleepers so that the horizontal flange faced outwards. The waggons, which had flangeless wheels, ran along the horizontal flange and were held in position by the

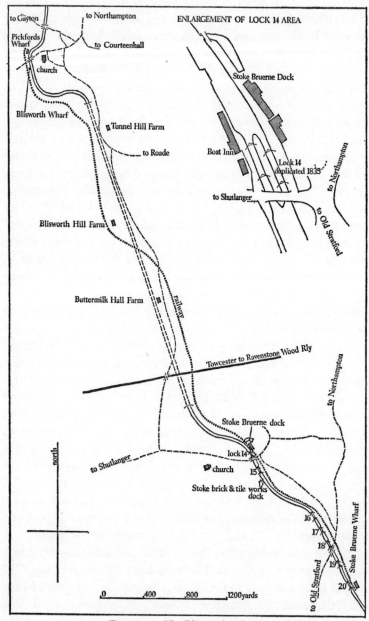

FIGURE 3. The Blisworth railway

upright flange.[8] From measurements taken the gauge was probably 4ft 2in, one favoured by Outram. A benefit was that as
flanged wheels were not required, ordinary waggons could be
used on the railway providing their gauge was right. Similarly,
elaborate sidings were unnecessary at the two termini as the
waggons could simply be run off the track and parked on a convenient piece of ground. It seems probable that the waggons
were hauled up the steeper parts of the line at either end in twos
or threes, and were then coupled together to form trains of about
a dozen behind a couple of horses.

During all this time work on the heading under the line of the
tunnel was still going on, but only on a small scale. Indeed, it
was not until the railway had been in operation for nearly a year
that, in November 1801, thoughts were again turning to the
tunnel for in that month the company advertised for proposals to
complete the work by contract. At the end of the month Jessop
and Barnes were asked to draw up a specification, together with
proper drawings and their estimates of the sort of prices that
ought to be paid if the work were carried out by contract. At the
same time an investigation was started into what quantities of
bricks and other materials which could be used for the tunnel
were already at Blisworth.

By January 1802 some preparations must have been going on
for brickmaking both at Blisworth and Stoke, as a complete halt
on all work was ordered, apart from turning the clay for brickmaking and on the deep cutting where five men were employed,
until Barnes had decided what should be let out to contract and
what the company should carry on with itself. In May Jessop's
plans for the tunnel were ready—the tunnel was to be 16½ft wide
with a total height of 18ft from the crown of the arch to the
bottom of the waterway. The side walls and the crown were to be
17in, or two bricks, thick and the inverted arch 13in, or 1½ bricks,
thick. Jessop thought that the contractor ought to be able to
finish the work in two years. He also recommended that wooden
slide rails should be fixed on both sides of the tunnel 6in below
water level and projecting 9in from the wall for the double

purpose of guiding boats through, particularly those with high loadings, but also, with the addition of wooden chocks fixed to the top of the rail every 9ft, to be used for pushing against for propelling boats through more easily than by pushing against the brickwork. Jessop estimated the cost of the rails at about £1,000.

Meanwhile Barnes had been valuing the work carried out by the company which he considered should be taken over and paid for by the contractor. The principal item was 600,000 bricks, which were valued at 31s 6d (£1.57½) per 1,000, and the list included sinking some of the pits, providing carts, centering, gins, timber, three brick kilns at Blisworth and one at Stoke, a total valuation of almost £2,100. Barnes also considered the contractor should take over three kilns at Stoke, owned by Joseph Ludlam who was making bricks for the tunnel. By far the most important work carried out by the company, however, was the driving of the main heading, and certain cross headings, to drain away the water. In all 610yd of heading had been driven at Blisworth at a cost of 36s (£1.80) per yard, and 2,012yd of heading and cross headings at Stoke at 42s 6d (£2.12½) per yard. In all, 2,218yd of heading had been driven parallel to the main tunnel. Barnes felt that this work should not be brought into the contract at all, but that it should be made clear that any cross headings still to be driven, together with the cost of clearing away the water, must be borne solely by the contractor.

It was decided to accept Jessop and Barnes' recommendations, and fresh advertisements were inserted in leading newspapers asking for proposals to complete the tunnel. All offers had to be in by 5 June, and shortly after the closing date it was decided to accept the tender submitted jointly by Jonathon Woodhouse, a civil engineer from Ashby de la Zouch, and his brother John, a civil engineer from Chilvers Coton, George Tissington, of Ashby, and his brother Anthony, a canal tunneller also from Ashby. Joseph Wilkes and William Hill of Measham agreed to join with the contractors in a £10,000 bond for the due completion of the work in two and a half years. Under the terms of the

Page 51 Two ornamental bridges: (above) Cosgrove; (below) Grove, Watford

Page 52   (*above*) Ice-breaking at the entrance of the Newport Pagnell Canal, Great Linford; (*below*) a horse-drawn boat at Fenny Stratford

contract the contractors agreed to build the tunnel in a 'good substantial and workmanlike manner' for £15 13s (£15.65) per yard, this price to include the oak rail recommended by Jessop. In addition they had to maintain the tunnel for one year after its completion. For its part the company agreed to advance £3,000 and to make stage payments as the work progressed against certificates from Barnes, but it was to retain £3,000 until the work was completed and a further £1,000 to the end of the maintenance period. If the contract was completed in two and a quarter years a £1,000 bonus was to be paid.

It seems that there was some delay before the contractors were able to start their work, and when they did they were hampered by poor weather. In September 1802 the company decided to allow them £1,000 per month for the next eight months. This followed a suggestion by Barnes that instead of devoting all their energies and their limited supply of bricks to the few pits where tunnelling had begun, the contractors rather should concentrate on getting all the pits sunk to the level of the tunnel and the first length of tunnel on either side of each pit completed. This was expected to be by far the most tedious and expensive part of the work, but Barnes felt that the final completion date could be brought forward by six months if this course were adopted. He realised, however, that the contractors would be at a disadvantage as the length of tunnel completed, on which the stage payments were based, would be small during this period. He therefore proposed that advances should be made based on the probable expenses to be incurred. Barnes calculated that £7,050 would be required over the eight-month period, but in addition fifty men would be employed in the deep cuttings at either end of the tunnel at a cost of £420 per month and a further £100 would be needed each month for horses, gins and other items. After 1 May 1803 the system of payment was to revert to the normal one against Barnes' certificates, with the contractors repaying the money advanced at the rate of £1,000 per month.

By November 1802, 134yd had been finished and the work was proceeding so well that it was confidently expected that the

D

tunnel would be opened well ahead of schedule.[9] In December Jessop recommended a major change of plan. As first proposed there were to have been two tunnels; the main one 2,900yd long in a straight line under the hill separated by a short curved cutting from a second 100yd long one at the Blisworth end. This course was suggested to allow the canal to follow the natural line of the valley at Blisworth and avoid a deep cutting through ground that appeared to be extremely treacherous for excavation and which contained several springs that would make it likely to slip. But Barnes had re-examined this proposal and found that if the main tunnel were extended slightly northwards the second tunnel could be dispensed with. It had been discovered that much of the soil thought to be treacherous was, in fact, good brick clay which was being used as such, whilst a heading driven on the north side of the cutting had succeeded in tapping the springs. Although a deep cutting of some 48ft would still be needed at the north end, Jessop agreed with Barnes' suggestions, but he recommended various measures to counteract any possibility of slips occurring. The contractors were then asked to execute this additional length on the same terms as the main tunnel, but at first they refused and asked for a higher price. This the company refused, threatening to give the work to another contractor who had offered to carry it out at a lower price. Eventually the company got its way.

By June 1803, 642½yd of the tunnel had been finished and the contractors appeared to be making excellent progress.[10] Towards the end of 1803 progress seemed to speed up with 77yd finished in August, 106½yd in September, 119yd in October, 121½yd in November and 145yd in December. Early in October there was an unfortunate accident when two workmen were killed. They were being hauled up one of the shafts in a basket, when the basket slipped off the hook and they fell back down the shaft, a depth of some 20yd. One of the men was killed instantaneously and the other survived only a few hours.[11]

Despite the apparent good progress being made with the work all was not well; for the company was becoming increasingly concerned by the amount of money advanced to the contractors.

These advances had been made to help them provide materials, and as they were used in the works so Barnes made due allowance in his certificates of work completed. Towards the end of 1803 Barnes was told to stop allowing for materials provided, and thereafter regular deductions were made from payments so as to repay the amount advanced by the company by the time the tunnel was expected to be finished.

Matters came to a head early in February 1804 when the company refused to honour a bill of exchange drawn by the contractors for over £1,930. This was reputedly for work on the main heading for which the company was paying under the terms of the contract, with the contractor being liable for the cross headings, but insufficient details of the work represented by the bill were provided. In the ensuing investigations heavy losses of up to £13,000 were disclosed by the contractors, who said they could not continue on the agreed terms and asked to be released from the contract. Part of the losses had arisen from quite unforeseen circumstances and the company made a payment of £2,400 as compensation, but the lion's share seems to have been due to sheer bad management by the contractors.

The company realised that to try and enforce the contract would probably merely involve a legal tussle for perhaps as long as a year, during which time the tunnel works would be at a standstill. It was decided, therefore, to dissolve the contract without more ado and to forego the £10,000 on the performance bond, as it was considered this would by no means compensate for delay to the tunnel works for any length of time. The contractors closed off their books as at 21 March 1804, when Barnes and two independent assessors valued the stocks of materials, equipment and work done. They put the length of tunnel completed at 1,618yd and noted the quality of the work done as being extremely high.[12] There was a last-minute effort by Jonathon Woodhouse and Edward Mammot, one of the independent valuers, to take over the contract but the company rejected their offer and ordered Barnes to assume full responsibility for all the tunnel works once again. At the same time Caleb Maullin was appointed as superintendent of trade at Blisworth, primarily to oversee the operation of the railway but also to give Barnes as much help as possible with the tunnel works, and he was entrusted with the purchase of materials.

Barnes appears to have entered into a series of small contracts with groups of workmen for them to carry out short lengths of the tunnelling work and in April 1804 he reported that two offers had been received to complete the tunnel by the end of February 1805 under contract. But the company must have felt that it had suffered enough with contractors and told Barnes that it would not agree to any major contract being let. In May John Woodhouse was appointed superintendent of the tunnel workmen.

Following the taking over of the works by the company the good rate of progress was not maintained to start with. This was mainly because most of the stocks of bricks had been used up as the weather had been unsuitable for making new bricks. The opportunity was taken, however, to complete the headings under the tunnel and an extra pit was sunk to give more working faces. The company seems to have been particularly unfortunate in its choice of contractors at Blisworth, for in June Joseph Ludlam, who had been carrying out various works, was put into prison at Northampton. Barnes had to measure up his work, which was mainly in the deep cuttings at either end of the tunnel, and arrange for someone else to take over so as to avoid any delay. Someone else who failed to come up to expectations was Maullin; he was dismissed in August 1804. Amongst other things he failed to keep proper accounts and Henry Provis was appointed in his place. In July a section of about 20yd of tunnel collapsed, giving rise to a certain amount of alarm in the area, but the fallen part was quickly replaced and as a precaution the brickwork was strengthened. In the same month Barnes was told to complete the two ends of the tunnel without delay. Thereafter the work seems to have gone ahead rapidly and comparatively smoothly with William Praed and other members of the committee keeping a close watch on progress. By September only about 980yd remained to be driven and four new pits had been sunk, whilst the brickmaking, which had held up the work before, was going very well.[13] In September 176yd were finished, with a further 226yd in October, bringing the total length up to nearly 2,500yd and leaving 570yd to be completed.[14] More would have been done but wet weather slowed the works somewhat. By the beginning of February only 88yd remained to be completed and the tunnel was finally finished on Monday, 25 February 1805.[15]

Meanwhile early in February 1804 thought was being given to the building of the Stoke Bruerne locks at the southern end of the tunnel, which would take the line down to the end of the railway and the stretch of canal already in use. A start was made by Henry Provis, and early in May orders were given for excavations for the foundations for two of the locks to be started. The locks were constructed mainly by contract. Initially William Jackson was working on them, but his rate of progress was unsatisfactory and he agreed to confine his efforts to just three of the locks from July 1804. Soon afterwards a contractor named Pashley from Buckingham agreed to build a further three and to take over the materials Jackson had already collected for them. By September the works were well advanced and the locks must have been completed at about the same time as the tunnel was finished.

As soon as the tunnel was completed Thomas Telford was invited to inspect it thoroughly, which he did in March. He reported that it was perfectly straight and the materials and workmanship were excellent.[16] The company then decided to hold the formal opening ceremony on Monday, 25 March 1805. A packet boat was ordered for the official party and a dinner for 100 people was provided at the Bull Inn at Stony Stratford at a cost of half a guinea each. The opening of the tunnel was a major event and a great crowd of people attended. The first boat through was the packet boat which went to join the other boats assembled at the north end to form a grand procession. For the occasion the darkness of the tunnel was relieved by a number of flambeaux and lights and the official party took one hour and two minutes to pass through to the south end where 5,000 people were gathered to greet them.[17]

The cost to the company of the second attempt at the tunnel was at least £90,000. Its length was 3,075yd 2ft and the 16½ft width meant that the usual narrow boats could safely pass inside. The height of the tunnel to the crown of the arch is 11ft 3in from water level, whilst the depth of water is 5ft 9in in the centre. Numbered cast iron markers were placed every hundred yards along

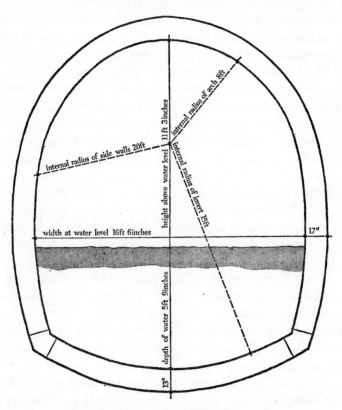

FIGURE 4.   Cross section of Blisworth tunnel

the west wall, with the numbering starting from the northern end. The wooden slide rails do not seem to have survived long and were eventually removed, probably because it was found they reduced the width of the tunnel too much. Also they offered a somewhat cumbersome way of working boats through compared to legging which now became standard (see Chapter 7). As the tunnel is perfectly straight it is possible to see through when it is not obscured by smoke or fumes.

There is no doubt that the building of Blisworth tunnel was a major undertaking for the engineers and contractors of the day. The first step in planning the work was to set out a straight line over the ground above the line of the tunnel, after which a longitudinal section was taken showing the rises and falls in that straight line. This section was then plotted to a suitable scale on paper and a straight line was drawn in to indicate the level of water in the tunnel underneath the ground contour. The longitudinal section was then divided into an equal number of parts and by scaling, the depth of the canal below ground level could be obtained at each point. Translating this to the actual ground gave the depth to which the shafts at each of the points should be sunk. Horizontal excavation along the line of the tunnel was then started in both directions from the foot of each shaft, and in due course all these excavations met, resulting in a straight and level tunnel. To set out a straight line $1\frac{3}{4}$ miles over Blisworth hill by sighting required one point high enough for the engineers to be able to see the full length of the line and at Blisworth the tunnel lines exactly on to the tower of St Mary's Church at Stoke Bruerne. This church stands on a high piece of ground, the view from the tower is extensive and it is almost certain that it was used as a sighting point for the tunnel. In all nineteen shafts were sunk, but most were filled in after the construction work had been completed. Initially four were retained as ventilating shafts and these are recognisable from the brick shafts on the ground above. The shafts look like chimneys and were built to create a draught as well as to prevent things falling down into the tunnel below. The sites of the filled in shafts can still be seen along the line of the tunnel as mounds some 100ft in diameter. These mounds were formed as earth was drawn up the shafts from the excavations below by horse-operated cranes, or gins as they were known.

The opening of the tunnel and the locks at Stoke Bruerne

meant that the railway over the hill and the transhipment facilities at both ends were redundant. Fortunately the company was able to re-use the expensive cast iron rails and many of the stone sleepers on the Northampton railway (see Chapter 4), but the carriers who operated over the line seem to have offered most of their rolling stock for sale. The company also sold much of the equipment used at the tunnel, disposing of 350 tons of cast and wrought iron, 5 mills for grinding brick clay, 14 pit gins with ropes, pulleys and many similar items.

Perhaps it was hardly surprising that a tunnel which had proved such a struggle to build could do anything else but go on to prove a constant headache to successive maintenance engineers of the company. The ground through which it was driven—clay, rock, limestone and ironstone—was extremely liable to move, particularly during wet weather, and these movements have caused serious distortions to the arch, walls and invert. In contrast, Braunston tunnel, only 18 miles away to the north, has always been comparatively trouble free and requires little attention.

The second handicap to the Grand Junction's through route once the canal was opened in 1800 was the temporary line across the valley of the river Great Ouse. Once the general line of the canal had been determined and the two summit levels, at Tring and Braunston, fixed, there was no alternative, without a long detour, to a series of locks into and out of the Great Ouse valley. In the original plans the canal was shown as crossing the river on the level between Old Wolverton and Cosgrove, the drop of some 190ft from Tring being achieved by some thirty-one locks and the rise of some 160ft to Braunston by another twenty-eight locks.

The Great Ouse has always been a river prone to flooding and it was realised that at times canal traffic might be seriously delayed at the river crossing. In December 1799 Barnes submitted a report on a proposed aqueduct over the river. The company saw what a major improvement this would be and ordered him to make an immediate start on the preparation of proper plans and to consult with the landowners who would be involved.[18] Barnes' proposals were soon agreed in principle, the cost being estimated at £25,000 with four locks on each side of the valley being eliminated. The decision was taken just in time for alterations to be incorporated in the plans for the canal between Stoke Bruerne and Little Woolstone so as to follow the contour and eliminate the locks.

In April 1800, when the company was making every effort to complete its through route, Jessop made a report in which he estimated that the aqueduct could hardly be completed in less than two years and so he recommended that a temporary canal should be constructed across the valley. The temporary line was to be on the upstream side of the proposed embankment with eight locks to overcome the drop of some 34ft from the level of the canal from Fenny Stratford to river level and the climb out again on the Cosgrove side. Jessop reported that these locks need not be made as substantially as permanent structures; the inverts could be of timber, saving some 80,000 bricks as well as the time and expense in laying them. It was then intended that the gates and other fittings would be transferred later to the Stoke Bruerne flight of locks, the construction of which had been deferred until Blisworth tunnel was completed. At the time of Jessop's report work was well advanced on building the canal proper from Fenny Stratford to Wolverton and from the end of the railway at Stoke Bruerne to Cosgrove, so construction of the temporary canal line across the valley was put in hand at once and was completed in September 1800.

With the opening of the through route no further action was taken over the aqueduct proposal until May 1802, when Jessop was asked to prepare a plan, section and estimate. Jessop forwarded his report in June and urged that the scheme be carried out as soon as possible.[19] It seems that there was a fair amount of local trade on the canal across the Ouse valley which needed a large amount of water from the Tring summit, where it could be ill afforded. To help cope with the situation whilst the aqueduct was under construction it was decided to build a 40-acre reservoir at Wilstone on the summit near Tring.

It was company policy at this time to let larger works to contract rather than carry them out itself by direct labour, and so the Wolverton scheme was put out to tender. At the end of November 1802 it was decided to accept the tender submitted jointly by Thomas Harrison of Wolverton, Major Mansel, Thomas and Joseph Kitchen of Castlethorpe and William Oliver of Stony Stratford. Their tender, based on Jessop's plans, was a price not exceeding 1s 3d (6p) for every cubic yard of earth, including the puddling, and a price not exceeding £12 for every rod of brick-work. The company's solicitors were told to draw up a draft contract for approval, whilst the contractors started getting their supplies of materials together. As an additional item the contractors were asked to undertake the widening of a narrow cutting at Old Wolverton. They also had to put up £5,000 deposit as surety.

By January 1803 Harrison, who was at one time the principal agent to Earl Spencer and who was the chief partner in the syndicate, had agreed to the terms of the contract and also to widen the narrow part of the canal at Old Wolverton at a rate of 2s 6d (12½p) per cubic yard. Harrison undertook to complete both jobs within two years. Work started immediately and in August 1803 the company appointed Henry Provis to superintend operations at Wolverton. It gave considerable assistance to the contractors, allowing them the use of the toll house and store at Cosgrove, and hiring out to them the railway lines, which had been bought for the proposed railway to Aylesbury, and several floats. It also agreed to contribute half the cost of a pumping engine needed to drain a section of the works.

It became apparent, however, early in 1804 that things were not going quite to plan, as Provis reported that the Wolverton Valley Company, as the contractors' syndicate was known, intended to make several extra charges for the work. The contractors were immediately asked for full details of these extras and Provis and Benjamin Bevan, an engineer from Leighton Buzzard, were told to prepare fresh estimates for the aqueduct and embankment, taking into account the extra charges. In April the figures prepared by Provis and Bevan were approved as the basis on which an agreement should be reached with the contractors.

Negotiations were started and agreement was reached in May, when the company's solicitors were told to amend the contract accordingly and to include in it Harrison's agreement to widen the cutting at Old Wolverton.

At the company's half yearly meeting in June 1804 the proprietors were told that two-thirds of the embankment and half of the aqueduct was finished, one-third of the work on the embankment having been carried out since the previous November. The contractors were trying to speed up progress and there seemed little doubt that the aqueduct would be ready in time for the opening of Blisworth tunnel. In October Harrison reported two variations from Jessop's plans in the work as it was being carried out; the length of the arch exceeded the plan by about 2ft and the backwalls of the arches and the abutments were 5ft high instead of 3ft. Perhaps Harrison could see signs of trouble ahead as he asked that due note should be taken of these variations to avoid any future disputes. In the same month Provis objected to the way the arches were being built and Charles Handley, who had engineered the Warwick & Napton Canal, was asked to inspect the work and to make a report. Provis was overruled, however, as Jessop had ordered the arches to be built in this way and presumably Handley agreed with him.

Work proceeded steadily but in April 1805 there was a disturbing newspaper report that the aqueduct had collapsed.[20] The committee met at once and issued a statement denying the report and declaring that Thomas Telford had just inspected the works and found everything satisfactory.[21] By the middle of August the works were at such an advanced state that a restricted channel was open over the aqueduct and embankment. As the water supply situation was again critical the company's treasurers proposed at a special committee meeting that the embankment should be opened for trade only until the beginning of November. The treasurers themselves undertook responsibility for the work in return for half of the additional tonnage revenue for the period. The contractors agreed to this suggestion and the aqueduct was opened for traffic on Monday, 26 August 1805.[22]

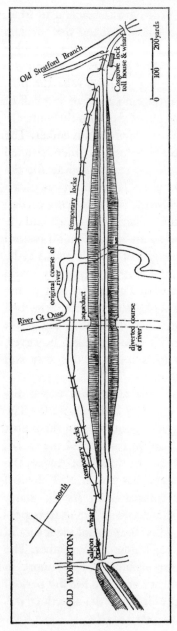

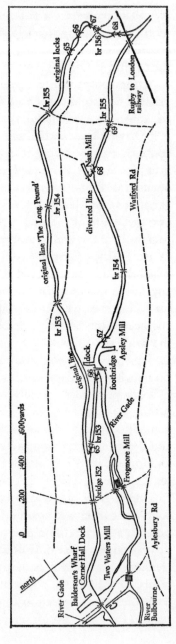

FIGURES 5 & 6.   Two deviations: (*above*) Wolverton valley; (*below* Apsley and Nash mills

Unfortunately, no plans of the aqueduct seem to have survived, but it was certainly a three-arched structure, the arches being semicircular and running under the full width of the embankment at river level, rather like enlarged culverts. The arches were constructed on dry land and the river was then diverted from its original course near to Cosgrove to pass through them. Even to this day gradual subsidence is taking place in the embankment over the old river course and it has had to be consolidated by timber piles driven into the slopes.

The aqueduct appears to have remained in use beyond the 1 November as originally proposed, but in January 1806 a section of the embankment near Cosgrove collapsed, almost certainly at the point of the old river crossing, putting an abrupt end to the water route over the valley.[23] A sub-committee was set up in February under William Praed's leadership to investigate the matter and decide on a suitable course of action, while John Rennie was called in to report on the state of the works. The sub-committee decided that the trouble had arisen through bad workmanship and a letter was sent to Harrison insisting on the company's right to have the works put into a proper state of repair and stating that the contractors would be liable for damages for the loss of trade suffered. Harrison's reply was rejected at a meeting in April and the case was referred back to the sub-committee for it to bring about a speedy settlement. But matters dragged on and on. The contractors claimed that the company was responsible for the repair of the damage as the work had been carried out in accordance with the contract and that there was still money due to them on account of the work done; and the company claimed that the works had never been properly completed and the contractors were liable not only to repair the damage but to compensate the company for the loss of traffic dues.

Matters were little further forward nearly a year later when, in June 1807, the committee heard from Harrison that as far as he was concerned the works at Wolverton had been completed long ago and that no further action was called for. Indeed, the contractors were, he said, withdrawing from the works on 1 July. The company then decided to seek outside assistance and called in a Mr Ware, an experienced architect, to report on the state of the works. Ware reported that the aqueduct was in a very dangerous and imperfect condition. The piers had sunk and were out of alignment and the counter arches had risen in the middle, whilst the whole structure had not been completed in accordance with the plans. At the same time Provis and Townley, an overseer, sent in a report about the embankment from which it seems that the contractors had made temporary repairs to the breach that had occurred in January 1806. However, a considerable amount of repair work still needed to be done, and the whole embankment, like the aqueduct, had not been finished to the specifications of the contract.

An ultimatum was then issued to Harrison stating that if his claims against the company had not been sent in by 29 September an action would be started to compel him and his fellow contractors to account to the company for the monies paid and advanced for the works. At long last, in October 1807, Harrison sent in his claim and Provis and Bevan were told to examine it with a view to reaching a speedy settlement. However, the dispute with the contractors took a dramatic turn when on the night of Thursday, 18 February 1808, the aqueduct collapsed. The *Northampton Mercury* of Saturday, 27 February, contained a full report of this famous disaster:

Stony Stratford. Feb 22.
On Friday morning last the inhabitants of this town were thrown into the utmost consternation, by information which arrived from Wolverton, that the large aqueduct arches under the immenseley high embankment for carrying the new line of the Grand Junction Canal across our valley, about a mile below this town, had fallen in; and that the river Ouse was so dammed up thereby, that this town must shortly be entirely inundated to a great depth. On repairing to the spot, however, it was found, that one of these arches, which had been propped up underneath with timber, soon after the centres were removed, was still standing; and that this one arch, owing to there being no flood in the river, was able to

carry off the water as fast as it came down. On examining the other two arches it appeared that about 22 yards in length of the middle part of each had fallen in, and blocked up the arches, laying the canal above in complete ruins, emptying it as far as the nearest stop-gate on each side, and exposing the remains of 500 quarters of coke and cinders, which the contractors had laid on the arches. The ends of each of the broken arches were found standing in a crippled state,—most fortunately for the public as well as the Company the old line of canal and locks across this valley are still standing, and in sufficient repair immediately to convey the barges, and prevent interruption to trade; but the loss of £400 a month, which we are told has of late been the amount of the extra tonnage received by the company for goods passing over this canal, will be lost to them during the period of rebuilding the arches and repairing the canal over them.

It seems that William Cherry, the toll clerk at Greenbridge lock, Cosgrove, was the first person to see the disaster and at 11 pm he had just time to let off some of the water before the embankment collapsed. He sent off a messenger to warn the inhabitants of Stony Stratford of the accident.[24] Fortunately there was only minor local flooding.

The Grand Junction committee met at once and were told that although the northern arch was still standing it was in a dangerous condition. On Jessop's orders the earth over the arch was removed and the men worked all day on Sunday on this vital task. Harrison was asked what steps he now proposed to take to reconstruct the aqueduct and Ware and Provis were asked to report on its condition and to submit plans for a new structure. A record of the loss of tonnage was also to be kept. Not unexpectedly Harrison declined to reconstruct the aqueduct on the grounds that the contractors were not responsible for the failure. Legal proceedings were then started against him.

The question of rebuilding the aqueduct was made all the more urgent by the large amount of trade on the canal and the dry weather, which was causing concern again in the long pound to Fenny Stratford where the water supply situation was serious. In April 1808 it was decided to erect a temporary wooden trunk across the breached aqueduct and an experienced carpenter named

Martyn signed an agreement to construct it. This was duly opened for traffic on Friday, 10 June 1808.[25] Its cost, together with the repairs to the canal, amounted to about £2,500, but in addition the company reckoned it had lost over £1,400 during the three and a half months the local trade across the valley had been stopped. Several years later Provis was awarded a gratuity of fifty guineas for his work in planning and superintending the erection of the wooden trunk.

In the meantime consideration was being given to the question of a permanent replacement. By May both Ware and Provis had completed plans for a new structure, but a decision on them was deferred. It seems that both these plans were for a conventional brick aqueduct, but the suggestion had been made that an iron aqueduct would be better and Bevan agreed with this view. After discussions it was decided to go ahead with this new idea and Bevan and Charles Harvey, the company secretary, were asked to make further detailed investigations. By September various aqueducts had been inspected, amongst them the Avon aqueduct on the Warwick & Napton Canal, the Longdon-on-Tern aqueduct on the Shrewsbury Canal, and Chirk and Pontcysyllte aqueducts on the Ellesmere Canal. Bevan had been able to make an estimate for an iron aqueduct at Wolverton and it was decided to approach two ironmasters, Reynolds and Hazeldine, to ask them to tender for the work.

Meanwhile the action against Harrison was proceeding, after the defendant had in vain attempted to promote a private settlement. The case was eventually tried before the Court of King's Bench on 18 July and after the trial had proceeded at some length it was agreed to refer the matter to William Boland, a barrister-at-law, to investigate the damage and the claims between the two parties.[26] By the beginning of November both sides had presented their case to the arbitrator and an award of £9,262 and costs was made to the company. The principal items in the award were in respect of the construction of the temporary wooden aqueduct, and the making of bricks at Stoke Bruerne for the new aqueduct amounting to £3,223. The company then approached Harrison for his proposals for settling the amount owing to it. Harrison proposed that the payment should be made in instalments, which was agreed, and it was finally decided that £2,500 would be paid on 1 January 1809, £2,500 on 1 April, £2,500 on 1 July and the balance on 1 October 1809, with interest on the last three instalments being charged from 1 January. In agreeing to these terms the company was undoubtedly trying to be helpful to Harrison, as it emerged during the trial that the failure of the works had been caused principally by the misconduct of various people employed and not by the contractor himself. Though, of course, ultimately responsible, he was utterly ignorant of the frauds being committed by people in whom he had trusted. The first instalment was paid punctually, but Harrison died on 9 March 1809. The settlement of his affairs took some time, but his son, who was his father's executor, undertook to repay the debt and in fact the remaining three instalments were repaid together about the end of June 1809.

In March 1809 a start was ordered on the work of collecting materials for building the pier of the new aqueduct and Bevan was asked to advise on the prices and quality of suitable stone which could be used. At the same time Reynolds and Hazeldine were asked for accurate prices for the iron castings. Both their tenders were considered early in April and that of Messrs Reynolds & Co of Ketley Iron Works accepted in principle. The contractors were required not only to supply and erect the ironwork, but also to maintain it for one year after it was completed. Meanwhile Bevan reported that he had found the gornall stone from Cornwall would be best for the pier, but later he found an equally suitable stone from the Hornton quarries in Warwickshire 1s 6d (7½p) per cubic foot cheaper and it was decided to use this instead. By May the plans had been finally decided and Reynolds was asked to submit a specification so that a contract could be drawn up.

Reynolds attended the next committee meeting, with his partner William Anstice, and offered to contract for the making and erection of the ironwork and to guarantee it for two years after

E

completion for £3,667.50. The company was to erect the pier and abutments for the aqueduct and to provide scaffolding, ropes and cranes. Reynolds' offer was accepted and work on the new aqueduct started in the autumn, the foundation stone being laid by Bevan on 9 September 1809.[27] Soon afterwards Bevan raised the question whether the two abutments, which were being built in brick, should be faced with stone to make them match the middle pier, which was being built entirely of stone. Bevan considered this was basically a matter of taste, with a saving of £250 if bricks were used. He was told to use bricks.

In November 1810 it was reported that the aqueduct was almost complete and it was finally opened for traffic on Tuesday, 22 January 1811 with but little ceremony, Bevan being accompanied across in the first boat by several gentlemen from Stony Stratford.[28] The total cost of the aqueduct and associated works was about £6,000. The structure has stood well and never threatened to repeat the disaster of 1808.

The dimensions of the aqueduct are 101ft 2in long, 15ft wide, 6ft 6¼in from top edge to floor inside and 35ft 7in from top edge to river level. There are two cattle creeps under the canal, one on each side of the river. These small tunnels, which were driven through the embankment to allow access to the other side of the canal, are 77ft long, 6ft high and 3ft 4in wide, whilst the arch is 9ft 9in below water level. The large lakes at the foot of the embankment on the north-east side were formed when material was excavated for the embankment. Little trace remains now of the eight temporary locks which were dismantled when the aqueduct was eventually functioning properly, but when piles were being driven in 1947 for a wharf at Old Wolverton the old timber invert of the top lock was encountered. The line of the foundations of the arches of the old aqueduct can still be seen in the river bed today.

CHAPTER 4

Building the Branches

ALTHOUGH projected primarily as a trunk waterway to shorten the distance between London and the industrialised Midlands, the Grand Junction Company was always anxious in its early days to link up with as many towns as possible by branch canals.

In the original Act four branches were authorised—from the Braunston summit level to the north-east of the town of Daventry, from Gayton near Blisworth to Northampton and the river Nene, from Cosgrove in Northamptonshire to run to the busy turnpike road at Old Stratford, and from near Rickmansworth to Watford in Hertfordshire. The Act also authorised the building of such feeders as might be needed to supply water to the main canal. But this was only a start, for at the company's first meeting Barnes was told to survey proposed branches to Aylesbury, Buckingham, Chesham, Dunstable, Hemel Hempstead, Newport Pagnell, St Albans and Wendover. Barnes had finished these surveys by early September when it was decided not to proceed with the Chesham, Hemel Hempstead and Newport Pagnell branches, the rest being passed over to Jessop for his opinion. He approved the plans and an Act was promoted to authorise all five. In December, however, it was decided not to proceed with the Dunstable branch in view of opposition from the landowners and this part of the Act was withdrawn. In the following February it was decided to delete that part of the Act relating to the St Albans branch as well, in view of anticipated opposition, and to bring in a separate Act for this branch in the next session of Parliament. The remaining three branches—from the Old Stratford branch to the town of Buckingham, from Marsworth to Aylesbury, and

71

from Tring to Wendover, this last being a feeder which was already being built under the powers of the first Act, were all authorised in the second Act,[1] which received the Royal Assent on 28 March 1794.

Towards the end of May 1794 it was decided to persevere with the St Albans branch, despite the expected opposition, and in June to bring in a Bill not only for this but also for a branch from Southall in Middlesex to Paddington on the outskirts of London. The Paddington line was authorised by an Act[2] which was passed on 28 April 1795, and despite the opposition the Act[3] for the line from Watford to St Albans received the Royal Assent on 2 June. These were the last successful Acts authorising branches until 1879 when the Slough branch was sanctioned.

Of all these branches those to Aylesbury, Buckingham, Northampton, Old Stratford, Paddington, Slough and Wendover were eventually built by the Grand Junction, whilst a canal to Newport Pagnell was built by an independent concern (see Appendix 3). The branches to Daventry, Watford and St Albans, although authorised by Parliament, were never built, whilst those to Hemel Hempstead, Chesham and Dunstable hardly got off the drawing board. In addition, several other proposals were made in the early days to link up with the Grand Junction, but none succeeded.

The navigable feeder to Wendover was the first branch to be completed, since there was at the time no other way of supplying the Tring summit with water. At the first committee meeting on 5 June 1793 negotiations were opened for the purchase of the Marquis of Buckingham's mill at Weston Turville and in July talks were started to buy a mill at Wendover. By this time Barnes had completed his detailed plans for the feeder and work started soon afterwards. By September the negotiations for the purchase of the mills, whose water was needed for the feeder, were almost complete, the Marquis of Buckingham's mill being bought for £400 and the Wendover mill for £1,750. An agreement had also been reached with Sir John Dashwood King for the purchase of the water rights to his mill at Halton and for his consent to the feeder passing through Halton village.

By the autumn of 1793 construction work was well under way. It being soon realised that little extra expense would be incurred in making the feeder navigable, powers to carry out this work were obtained in the 1794 Act. In May 1794 the company rejected a suggestion that the branch should be extended further into Wendover, proposing instead that a road from the town should be built. Otherwise the work proceeded uneventfully and the 6¾ mile long level branch was completed probably sometime in 1796. It was certainly finished by March 1797.[4]

The next to be built were the Old Stratford and Buckingham branches. In the deposited plans they are shown as running from the junction with the main canal and the river Great Ouse up the valley first to the Roman road, Watling Street, at Old Stratford, and then on up to Buckingham. It was intended to make the Buckingham branch chiefly by canalising the river and climbing the valley by a series of locks. The only cut of any length was between the main line junction and the village of Passenham, with the canal running in practically a straight line to Watling Street and then sweeping round in a gentle curve to pass close to Passenham church before rejoining the river. After that the course of the river was followed to Buckingham, with some of the worst bends being straightened by short cuts. The reason for following the river must have been to reduce the engineering works and to ensure a constant supply of water for the two branches.

When the decision was taken that the main canal should cross the Ouse valley on an aqueduct, the plans for the branches had to be altered, and a new junction with the main line was selected at the north end of the embankment. As this point was nearly 40ft above river level at the aqueduct the need for all but two of the locks on the Buckingham branch was eliminated. The amended line now followed the contour up the valley until contact was made with the river for a short distance above Maids Moreton mill.

In its early days considerable pressure was put on the Grand Junction by the various towns to which branches were proposed

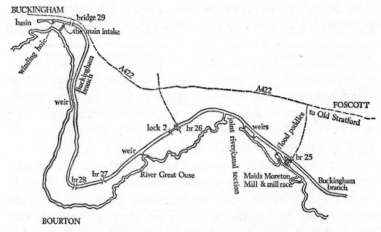

FIGURE 7.　The upper section of the Buckingham branch

for priority in the construction programme and it is probable that Buckingham would have been well down the list had it not been for the Marquis of Buckingham, who lived at Stowe near the town. In May 1800 the Marquis agreed to lend the company the estimated amount needed to build the branch from Old Stratford to Buckingham. The Marquis asked for the work to be carried out as quickly as possible and Barnes was told to start as soon as he could. Indeed, once the labour force had finished its work on cutting the main line in August 1800 they went straight on to complete the Old Stratford branch which, with its short length of 1¼ miles and relative freedom from engineering works, was a cheap and easy affair to construct. It also had the important connection with Watling Street, which gave it considerable traffic potential. The Old Stratford branch was finished in either August or September 1800 and work then started on the 9½ miles long Buckingham branch, which was completed in the very short time of eight months:

the Branch of Canal from Buckingham to the Grand Junction Canal was opened for trade on the first of May (1801) with great rejoicings. A barge with the Marquis of Buckingham, Mr. Praed, and Mr. Selby (Gentlemen of the Committee) and Mr. Box the

Treasurer, accompanied by a large party of Ladies and Gentlemen, and a band of music, led the way to a procession of twelve barges laden with coals, slate and a variety of merchandise. Upon their entry into the Bason at Buckingham they were saluted by the firing of several pieces of cannon.[5]

The branches became of great importance to Buckingham and the surrounding district and were soon carrying 20,000 tons each year. The district was mainly agricultural, and one of the principal reasons for the building of the Buckingham branch was for the export of hay and straw for the thriving horse-drawn traffic of London. In return, coal, stone and other goods could be supplied to the area with a tremendous saving in price over other forms of transport.

As trade began to develop on the main canal it did not take the company long to realise that its connection with the Thames at Brentford was not ideally placed to attract much of the considerable trade to and from many parts of London. The company did its best to increase its trade through Brentford by opening a wharf on the Thames at Whitefriars, above Blackfriars Bridge. Land had been purchased there in July 1794 and Jessop had reported on the buildings that would be needed. In May 1795 it was decided to build a covered wet dock together with a two-storey warehouse and the works were probably completed and the wharf opened early in 1796. Later in the year increasing trade necessitated an extra storey to be added to the warehouse and other improvements made, until, by the early 1800s over £28,000 had been invested in the facilities. But despite the success of the wharf, the advantages to be gained by building a branch canal to extend the line nearer to London could not be overlooked.

In May 1794 Jessop and Barnes carried out a survey for a branch to London and selected Paddington for the termination of such a line. At the time Paddington was ideally situated on the edge of the built-up part of the capital and it had the advantage that it could be linked with the nearest convenient point on the main line by a level branch. Jessop and Barnes' outline plans were adopted in June, when it was decided to go ahead and apply for an Act.[6] Barnes completed more detailed plans by the beginning of September and the Act was obtained in the following year with relatively little trouble, as the scheme had overwhelming public advantages. Indeed the Paddington branch was soon to become by far the most important and economically successful of all the Grand Junction's extensions.

In June 1795 Jessop produced a report on the best way of building the branch, but nothing was done, since efforts were then being concentrated on the main canal. Funds were also being conserved for this purpose; indeed in June 1796 it was decided that no money should be spent on branch canals unless funds were subscribed specifically towards their construction.[7] But so important was the Paddington line that £5,000 was set aside for work on a deep cutting and embankment near the river Brent.[8] Barnes and Gream, a surveyor, were then told to set out the line of the branch and in October 1796 the company decided to issue 500 new shares of £100 each so that a start could be made on the work without entrenching on the money available for the all-important main line.[9] In November land purchases started and construction work began soon after.

June 1797 saw the setting up of a special committee under the chairmanship of Edmund Dayrell to supervise the work and in November Barnes was able to report that a mile and a quarter of the line was finished and full of water, upon which six floats were in use carrying earth from Horsendon Hill to the valley over the Brent. Bricks were also ready for the aqueduct over the river and for those bridges that were to be built next summer. But whilst the works were proceeding steadily the negotiations for land purchase were not. In February 1797 disagreements with the Bishop of London over land at Paddington were reported and this was the start of a protracted wrangle. In August, as the problem seemed as intractable as ever, consideration was being given to diverting and extending the line from Kensal Green either to Marylebone or some other point further into London. By 13 September Parliamentary notices had been given for no less than three possible routes for the extension, as the company had been unable to decide which would be the best. The proprietors approved this action in November, provided an agreement could not be reached with the Bishop and his lessees, and authority was given to go ahead with an application to Parliament. Perhaps this provided the spur, for in December outline proposals for an agreement with the Bishop were submitted and in April 1798 Praed was authorised to conclude it.

In May 1799, somewhat belatedly perhaps, Gream was told that in his negotiations with landowners he should purchase a 96ft wide strip of land wherever possible. This was to allow for a double towing path, which had been authorised in the Act, and in October Barnes was told to provide this. But in April 1800 both Jessop and Barnes agreed that no good purpose would be served by a double path, beyond that already built, in view of the considerable extra cost. The earlier decision was then reversed, with a single path being ordered between Southall and the Brent aqueduct. Meanwhile in June 1799 plans were started for the buildings at the end of the branch at Paddington and it seems these plans soon became so ambitious that negotiations had to be reopened with the Bishop of London for more land. By March 1800 these talks were under way and Barnes was told to stop all work southwards from the Brent aqueduct until an agreement had been reached and to use his labour force on finishing the embankments and other works on the branch.

In April Jessop reported that the line from Southall to the Brent valley was finished and from there to Paddington work was progressing well, except at the embankment near the river and the deep cutting immediately to the south. He thought if about 220 men could be kept on those parts of the canal it could be open to Paddington by Christmas. Six months later a fair amount remained to be done and Barnes was having to make more bricks at Alperton. But the end was in sight, for on 21 February 1801 Barnes was told to set out the line of the end of the branch at Paddington so that the committee could inspect and finally decide at a meeting three days later. At this meeting the line from the Harrow Road bridge to the terminus was settled and work started

immediately with the excavated soil being used to form the base
of the wharves at Paddington. At the same time the company
started advertising that it was willing to let land at Paddington
for wharfage, warehousing and other purposes. Work on the
final stretch was soon finished and the branch was opened on 10
July 1801:

> Yesterday sennight the canal to Paddington was opened for trade
> with a grand procession along the Paddington line to Bulls Bridge
> at Uxbridge. Exactly at nine o'clock, the Committee, with their
> Friends, in two pleasure boats, set sail with colours and streamers
> flying, each vessel being towed by two horses. At twelve o'clock
> the Company were met at Bulls Bridge by the City shallop and
> several pleasure boats.
> . . . on meeting a salute was fired and then the procession re-
> turned. At half after five o'clock the cavalcade reached the Great
> Dock. This was announced by the firing of cannon, on West-
> bourn-Green Bridge and a volley of musketry from the town.[10]

Even before the branch was opened it was realised what a
tremendous asset the canal could be for water supply purposes.
On October 1794 an approach was made by the Duke of Portland,
who was at the time concerned with a plan to supply parts of
Marylebone with water. Nothing came of this, but it must have
prompted the company to consider if it could not undertake the
supply itself, for at the time many parts of London were without
a piped supply and there was considerable scope for enterprise.
Indeed, when an Act[11] was obtained on 26 May 1798, principally
to confirm the agreement with the Bishop of London, powers
were granted which enabled the Grand Junction to set up as a statutory water undertaker. In October 1799 a union with the Chelsea
Waterworks Company was considered but no agreement was
reached and a similar approach once the branch was opened also
got nowhere; neither did one to the New River Company in 1801
nor to the West Middlesex Company in 1808. Once the branch
was opened, work on the water supply side went ahead and this
activity soon became an important side line; so much so that it
was transferred to a separate undertaking, the Grand Junction

Water Works Company, by an Act[12] in 1811. This company remained in being until the Metropolitan Water Board was set up in 1902, when it was absorbed along with other water supply concerns in London. Since 1820, however, the Water Works Company had ceased to draw their supplies from the Paddington branch, apparently owing to complaints about its quality.

The scheme for the Paddington branch had a forerunner some years before the Grand Junction project materialised. In 1766 a canal was proposed from the river Colne at Drayton to Marylebone, but shortly afterwards the western end was amended to join the Colne at Uxbridge, whence canals to other parts of the country were visualised. For much of its course the line of this proposed canal followed the contour to avoid lockage and was very similar to the Paddington branch. In 1773 there was a proposal to extend this canal across the north of London to Moorfields, where there was to have been a large basin on the site of present day Finsbury Circus, whilst another plan was for a further extension to the river Lee at Waltham Abbey.[13]

Consideration was given at an early stage to extending the Paddington branch still nearer to the City of London. Initially prompted by the disputes with the Bishop of London, later the scheme was considered on its own merits for its considerable commercial advantages. In 1800 a suggestion was made to extend the branch to Tottenham Court Road but in February the company decided that the drop of 30ft in level could give rise to considerable problems. In 1802 Thomas Homer was investigating a canal from the branch at Paddington to the Thames at Limehouse[14] and a railway to the docks was also considered at this time. John Rennie did a survey, and although no action resulted at the time, out of the idea grew the Regent's Canal, which was authorised in 1812 and opened on 1 August 1820. This canal joined the Paddington branch about three-quarters of a mile from its end. At first the Regent's had tried to negotiate with the Grand Junction for a supply of water, but as the talks were unsuccessful an Act of 1816 authorised it to draw water from the Thames at Chelsea. By an agreement of 1819, however, this supply was transferred to the Grand Junction Water Works Company and in exchange the Regent's obtained water rights from the Grand Junction.

The transformation at Paddington, which prior to the opening of the branch had been a quiet rural community, was remarkable, for almost overnight there developed a thriving inland port. The company was not slow to develop the land it owned in the area and its property interests soon became a profitable sideline. A very large amount of trade was soon passing over the Paddington wharves. In 1810 113,220 tons were received and 67,728 tons despatched by the branch. Apart from general goods the most important inwards cargo was bricks for the building trade, which was heavily involved in the rapid expansion of the capital at the time. At its western end the branch passed through excellent clay bearing land and several brickyards were established in the Hayes and Southall areas, many of which were served by private branch canals. Other typical items handled were manufactured goods from the Black Country, stone from quarries in Leicestershire and salt from Cheshire. Exports from Paddington included many of the waste products of the capital such as ashes, breeze and manure.

Indeed, with the opening of the branch the whole commercial emphasis shifted away from Whitefriars and soon afterwards Pickfords, the carriers, leased much of that installation. In June 1803 the disposal of the wharf was being considered, but was deferred. Later, in December 1809, part of the wharf was sold but the rest was retained as an investment property. When the Regent's Canal was opened, some trade was diverted from Paddington to such places as the City Road Basin, which was more centrally placed, but Paddington retained an important share and the branch itself was just as busy, as the diverted trade still passed along it on its way to or from the Grand Junction main line.

Once the branch was opened the company experimented with a regular passenger service from Paddington to Uxbridge, initially with a single boat, but later with a further two craft. The boats were named *Royal George*, *Marquis of Buckingham* and *William Praed*. On 23 July 1801 it was ordered:

the Steersman of the Passage Boat to be provided with a Blue
Waterman's Jacket with Yellow Stand-up-Cape and a double Row
of Yellow Buttons and that the Postillions be also provided with
Blue Jackets with Yellow Stand-up-Capes with plain Yellow
Buttons and to have Yellow Badges on the left Arm with the
letters GJC thereon.

The boats made a useful profit; for the 18 months from 24
June 1801 a surplus of £2,709 was shown, but thereafter the
return declined and in May 1803, probably to save itself the bother
of running the service, the company leased the boats to Henry
Weeks for seven months for £500 and 25 per cent of the takings
over £1,000. In January 1804 Thomas Homer leased the boats for
three years at £750 per annum, and in 1807 the lease was renewed
for another five years at £500 per annum. The regular services then
petered out and thereafter the only passengers carried from
Paddington were on excursion trips, which became quite popular
at one time. Soon after the opening of the branch there was also a
private passenger and goods service from Paddington to Buckingham, but this did not survive long.

Although one was authorised in the original Grand Junction
Act, it was to be many years before the inhabitants of Northampton were able to enjoy a connection by water with the canal. In
the deposited plans the branch was to have left the main canal
some distance north from the present junction and run down a
natural valley in a north-easterly direction to link up with the
present line at the bottom of the Rothersthorpe flight of locks. In
1796, however, Barnes was told to make another survey and in
October he reported that £25,349 would be needed to construct
the branch:

	£
8,060yd of common cutting and puddling	3,224
116ft of lockage	12,760
Bridges	1,890
38 acres of land at £60 per acre	2,280
Cutting and embankment at head and tail of locks	920
Fencing, culverts, weirs, buildings and damages	2,507
Contingencies	1,768

Barnes' estimate was somewhat higher than an earlier one by Jessop. He explained the difference by higher costs for land and building materials, making the locks 6ft longer and the need for extra fencing. Even at this stage a railway had been suggested as an alternative to the branch canal, but Barnes refrained from commenting on this, apart from mentioning the obvious disadvantages of transhipment at either end. No action on the report was taken and an estimate from Outram early in 1798 for a railway from Blisworth to Northampton was similarly shelved.

Early in 1800 the commissioners in charge of the river Nene navigation, who were becoming alarmed at the loss of trade on their river, approached the company with an offer to raise the money so that the branch could be built at once. The company agreed to build a railway if Northampton found the money and Jessop was told to make a survey. His report was issued in April and he estimated the cost of a single track railway from Gayton to Northampton at £9,000. He did not recommend this, however, as he considered the line would be out of action for weeks at a time owing to floods in the low-lying meadows it would have to cross near the town. Jessop proposed a part canal, part railway scheme. From Gayton he advocated a level canal about five-eighths of a mile long, then a railway falling on a gradient of 1 in 72, and finally a canal into Northampton by the Parliamentary line for 2¾ miles with three locks, each having a fall of 8ft. The locks would be 10ft wide and 100ft long so as to accommodate two Nene barges. The whole scheme was estimated as costing £12,975, comprising £1,040 for the upper canal, £7,123 for the lower canal, £3,120 for the railway and cranes, and £1,692 for contingencies at 15 per cent. If a single track railway were adopted there would be a saving of £1,120, making the total £11,855. Jessop envisaged that one horse would be able to work the railway in normal times and that it could cope with 20,000 tons each year.

The Nene commissioners, at a meeting in April, reluctantly approved Jessop's plans, feeling it would be far better to have a canal all the way, and another meeting was called for 8 May to

receive subscriptions to pay for the work.[15] £12,000 was being
sought, at 5 per cent interest, but the money was not forthcoming
and so no action was taken by the Grand Junction. Something of
a feud then developed between the company and the town of
Northampton, which smouldered for several years. In October
1802, at a public meeting with Lord Northampton in the chair, a
strong resolution was passed in favour of the canal being cut.[16] At
this time the company was applying for an Act to enable it to
raise more money and Northampton was opposing it unless the
company would agree to build the branch to the Nene. And so on
18 November, when the public meeting was resumed, the company came forward with an offer to build a level canal from
Gayton, and from the end of this a railway to Northampton, the
work to be completed by June 1804.[17] The meeting rejected this
plan and demanded the branch canal as specified in the original
Act. This demand was in turn rejected by the company, who
pointed out that for the time being an adequate water supply
simply could not be obtained for the branch. At the request of the
Nene commissioners proposals for overcoming the water shortage by reservoirs were then considered, but apparently these were
not satisfactory, for after further negotiations the company
decided, with the agreement of the commissioners, in February
1803 to build the part canal part railway line, the work to be
finished by 25 March 1805.[18] Sufficient money was to be ear-
marked for this scheme from the money now to be raised by the
company to complete its other works and a provision to this
effect was inserted in the Act.

Following this agreement with Northampton Barnes and
Barker, another surveyor, were told to prepare detailed plans
for the branch. At first it seemed that the old idea of the railway
linking two sections of canal would be revived, but in August
1803 a level canal from Gayton was specified and then a single-
track railway with proper passing places down to Northampton.
Sufficient land was to be taken for a double line. In November
1804, however, Barnes was told to make the line a railway
throughout, probably in an attempt to keep the cost as low as

possible. Despite the time limit imposed by the 1803 Act little seems to have been done until the end of 1804. But after the opening of Blisworth tunnel in March 1805 the materials from the double-track railway over the top of the tunnel were used on the Northampton line, supplemented by other rails the company had been using at Wolverton, and the work was finished and the railway opened on Monday, 7 October 1805[19] at a cost of about £12,000. Except at the Gayton end the line followed the course of the present day canal. From the top lock, however, a more direct course than the present one was taken to the main canal. At the junction itself the railway terminated alongside a small basin, which had been constructed out of the main canal to handle traffic for Northampton.

But the railway did not satisfy the people of Northampton, and when the company obtained a further Act in 1805 authorising increased tolls a special clause was inserted exempting the railway until such time as the branch canal was completed. Northampton continued to express its dissatisfaction and it seems that the railway was not entirely satisfactory for all types of goods. In May 1807 two carriers announced the establishment of a land carriage between Blisworth wharf and Northampton, for whilst the railway was suitable for carrying coals it was found inconvenient to use it for such things as grain and timber. In 1809 Northampton Corporation claimed the railway was inadequate, that the line was more difficult and expensive than a canal, that articles conveyed were subject to breakage and pilferage and that all perishable articles were prevented from passing along it.

Towards the end of 1809 the promoters of the Grand Union Canal, which was projected to link the unfinished Old Union Canal with the Grand Junction at Norton, were becoming active. It was hardly to be expected that Northampton would welcome this proposal, as it would finally rule out any possibility of the Old Union ever completing its extension to the Nene. In December it was decided to oppose the Grand Union Bill and at the same time to renew pressure on the Grand Junction, which was one of the main sponsors behind the Grand Union project, for the

Page 85 Blisworth tunnel: (*above*) leggers emerging; (*below*) reconstructing the north portal in 1903

Page 86 Tunnels: (*above*) a steam tug leaving Braunston; (*below*) the Blisworth brushing boat

early completion of the Northampton branch. In January 1810 the Grand Junction finally capitulated and agreed to complete the branch canal in three years,[20] much to the jubilation of Northampton whose opposition to the Grand Union Bill was withdrawn, but as the branch was planned with narrow locks to save money and water a clause was inserted to the effect that if ever the locks at Watford and Foxton on the new canal should be widened the locks on the Northampton branch must also be widened. It would seem that the Nene commissioners had agreed to assist with the financing of the work against a Grand Junction guarantee of 5 per cent on the sum lent, with any balance from the tolls going to the company. In June 1812 it was estimated that £35,000 would be needed to complete the branch.

Nothing seems to have been done until the summer of 1812 when stocks of bricks started to be collected, the sites of the locks were worked out and plans were made to cause as little interference with the railway as possible. In August 1813 Benjamin Bevan, who had been placed in charge of the works, reported on the progress made. The foundations of the bottom lock were nearly complete and the canal across the meadows in Northampton to the next lock, was cut and puddled. The bricks were ready on site for seven locks with some provided for another two locks, whilst a further million bricks were in store at Gayton and more were being made. Half the oak timber had been provided and 20,000ft of sawing done. Two lime kilns had been built and were in use and other materials had been collected in readiness. By June 1814 completion was hoped for by the end of October, as Bevan was able to report that all the cutting had been done except for 1⅜ miles, seven of the seventeen locks were finished, the bricks for all the rest were ready on site, all the lockgates had been framed and the iron work was finished on several of them. In November, however, the work still had some way to go. Seven locks and over half a mile of cutting had to be completed and whilst all the lockgates were finished only one-third had been hung and fitted. Seven bridges had been finished, with another six remaining to be completed. A revised opening date was now the beginning of

F

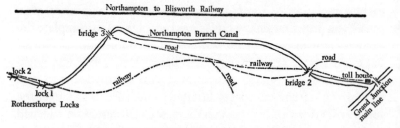

FIGURE 8.   The Northampton railway at Gayton

March. Even this was optimistic, for it was not until Monday, 1 May 1815 that the $4\frac{7}{8}$ mile long branch was finally opened. On that day a great crowd gathered to see the first boats arrive, twenty of which were carrying coals and the others all sorts of merchandise from various parts of the country.[21]

The canal was an immediate success and was soon carrying a considerable volume of traffic. Grain to mills on the river Nene was always an important commodity as was leather goods and straw board for the shoe trade in Northampton. Another important traffic at one time was ironstone to the works at Hunsbury Hill. This was mined around Blisworth and transported on waggon ways to the Grand Junction main line where it was loaded into boats. These boats then descended the branch to Hunsbury Hill where they were unloaded on to another set of waggons. There was a winding hole just below Hunsbury Hill lock, known appropriately as Furnace lock, where the boats turned for the journey back to Blisworth.

The cost of the branch is believed to have been £35,382. Little is known about the fate of the railway, but in December 1816 there was a sale of some wooden blocks taken from the line, whilst in 1824 the company was trying to dispose of other materials to the Thames Tunnel and the engineer was offered items at $4\frac{1}{2}$ guineas per ton. In 1825 it was decided to get rid of the rails lying at Gayton and a price of £6 10s (£6.50) per ton was asked for them.

Aylesbury found itself in a very similar position to Northampton in that it took many years to get its branch, authorised in

1794, built. No action was possible at first, for it was not until the end of the 1790s that the main canal was open to Marsworth, where the branch canal to Aylesbury was to start. In August 1800 certain people from Aylesbury approached the company saying that enough money had been promised to cover the estimated cost of a railway to the town and asking the company to go ahead with this work. The company agreed and ordered the cast iron rails that would be needed, but in November there was a change of plan and Barnes was told to use the rails that had arrived at Wolverton until they were needed for the Aylesbury line. Probably the reason for the delay was that at about this time suggestions were being made for extending the Aylesbury branch to Abingdon. Acting on behalf of a group of subscribers led by the Wilts & Berks Canal Company a survey was carried out by one of the Wilts & Berks engineers, but at first the Grand Junction was only mildly interested. This may well have been because it was expected to find the water for the new canal from the Grand Junction and as the main canal was none too well supplied at the time this probably also explains why the company was keen to adopt a railway.

In April 1802 Barnes was told to re-survey the line of a railway to Aylesbury and in May John Holland, a surveyor, started on the work between Aylesbury and Broughton mill. But little was actually done, for early in 1803 Jessop made a report and in March it was decided that it would be better to have a branch canal after all.[22] John Barker was then told to survey a canal line and try to find some means of saving water by reducing the lockage. In June Barnes and Holland were called in to assist with this survey. But still nothing was done, although contact was maintained with the Wilts & Berks, and the people of Aylesbury were becoming restless at the lack of progress. In February 1805 the company agreed to build a canal or a railway to Aylesbury as soon as possible provided extra money could be raised to supplement the original amount raised in Aylesbury but which was now insufficient. A group of the original subscribers met in November and threatened to take legal action, but the company was not to be moved. Undeterred, the people of Aylesbury went ahead and in the autumn of 1806 preparations were being made to introduce an Act to force the Grand Junction to make the branch canal and to apply the sum of £20,256 towards the work as the company had promised.[23] But the Bill did not succeed.

In 1808 the Marquis of Buckingham proposed a canal to run from Seabrook, not far from Marsworth, to Thame and in August the company agreed to support the project with a £15,000 loan spread over three years. But various conditions were imposed, mainly over the all-important water supply situation, and the Marquis, on learning of these conditions, decided not to proceed. In October 1809 the link with the Wilts & Berks came up again with an approach from that company. The Aylesbury to Abingdon scheme, now known as the Western Junction Canal, was strongly supported by Aylesbury. As was the case with the Northampton branch, matters came to a head with the Grand Union Bill. The Marquis of Buckingham and several people in Aylesbury petitioned against this and only agreed to withdraw their opposition in exchange for an undertaking by the Grand Junction to build the Aylesbury branch. Eventually an agreement was reached in March 1810 that if both the Grand Union and the Western Junction Bills passed through Parliament, the Grand Junction would agree to the Western Junction making the branch from Marsworth to Aylesbury, as part of the line to Abingdon. If the Western Junction Bill failed but the Grand Union Bill passed the Grand Junction agreed to make the branch to Aylesbury within a certain time. But if neither Bill passed the Grand Junction agreed to make a railway to Aylesbury unless a later agreement could be made with the Marquis for a canal to Thame. Following this agreement the Grand Junction got down to serious study of the Western Junction plan and an agreement with the Wilts & Berks was made in March 1810. The line, as surveyed by Barker, Whitworth and Provis, was approved, the estimate being £200,000, of which £70,000 each was to be found by the Grand Junction and Wilts & Berks shareholders and the remaining £60,000 from the general public. Water was still a crucial factor and the Grand Junction insisted that no lock should have a fall greater than 6ft. As planned, the line was to run from Marsworth to Aylesbury and then through Stone, Long Crendon and Cuddesdon to join the Wilts & Berks near Abingdon.

Considerable opposition came from the Kennet & Avon Canal Company, which was promoting a rival canal. This was from near Maidenhead to Cowley and had its origin in 1795 when in August a suggestion was made to the Grand Junction for a canal from Cowley to Boulters lock on the Thames in order to bypass a particularly treacherous stretch of the river. Little more was heard of the plan for a time but at the end of May 1801 Holland was told to survey a canal from Cowley to the Thames at Marlow, with a branch to Reading, again with a view to cutting out difficult stretches of the river. Holland worked in collaboration with Barnes and in May 1802 Peter Potter was appointed to assist him with the surveying and measurement work. In June the company decided to apply for Parliamentary powers for such a canal and by September Holland had completed his plans. He made three proposals for canals: from Cowley to the Thames near Marlow, from Cowley to the Thames at Sonning passing through Maidenhead, and from Cowley to the river Kennet at Reading. In November the third scheme was selected, and the application to Parliament was re-affirmed.

Opposition to the scheme was not slow to develop, coming from landowners, whose property would be affected, and from the Thames Navigation Commissioners, who were largely landowners themselves. Several well-supported meetings were held by the opponents and, faced with this formidable barrage of hostility, the company decided discretion was the better part of valour and withdrew the Bill for the time being. The company hoped the landowners would have second thoughts but it was also influenced by lack of support from the Kennet & Avon, which probably had enough on hand in trying to complete its own canal. The scheme was revived in 1810 by the Kennet & Avon, who proposed three schemes to bypass stretches of the Thames:

a canal from the Kennet at Reading to the Thames at Cookham and then from the Thames at Boulters lock to the Grand Junction at Cowley, from the Kennet at Reading to the Thames at Isleworth, and from the Kennet & Avon Canal near Newbury to the Basingstoke Canal near Basingstoke. The Grand Junction was approached for support and replied that before a firm decision could be given it would have to know which of the three schemes was to be adopted; it was also concerned to know the reaction of the landowners. No further action appears to have been taken at the time on any of the proposals, but the project for the canal from Boulters lock to Cowley continued to be discussed and became known as the Western Union Canal.

The defeat of the Western Junction Bill meant that Aylesbury was no nearer getting its branch canal built. In March 1811 the Marquis of Buckingham and certain others interested met the Grand Junction and agreed that the branch to Aylesbury should be started at once, the work being financed by calls on Western Junction shareholders. The money so subscribed was to be regarded as a loan and if Parliament later authorised the Western Junction Bill it could be converted into shares. In that case the Aylesbury branch was to be handed over to the new company. A limit of £20,000 was set on the money to be raised in this way, with the agreement expiring in August 1812, by which date the Grand Junction became liable to construct the branch as agreed in March 1810. In August 1811 Thomas Tindall, a solicitor in Aylesbury who had been very active in trying to get the branch built, wrote saying that £1,300, the first instalment of the loan, had been paid into a local bank, and on 13 August a start on the work was ordered with Henry Provis in charge.

Work proceeded slowly and in August 1813 Provis reported that nearly a mile of the canal from Marsworth was navigable through seven locks, with a further $3\frac{1}{2}$ miles completed from the Aylesbury end through another four locks. Three-quarters of the remaining mile and a half of cutting had been started and of the remaining five locks to be built two had been started. Ten of the eighteen bridges had been finished and two more were nearly complete. To the end of July nearly £24,000 had been spent on the works, excluding land purchases, and a further £18,000 would be needed to finish the branch.

Meanwhile the Western Junction proposal had not been dormant. In September 1813 notices appeared for a projected Aylesbury & Abingdon Canal, to run from the Thames at Culham to Aylesbury, with a branch to Wotton Underwood to improve the water supply position. There were to be reservoirs at Stoke Mandeville and Ellesborough and another branch to Chalgrove was suggested, again to act as a water feeder. At a public meeting in Thame in September with Lord Nugent in the chair, it was announced that the estimate, excluding the Chalgrove branch, was £191,800.[24] A committee was appointed, but there was no mention of taking over the Aylesbury branch as had been intended in March 1811. But like the Western Junction this scheme came to nothing.

Work on the Aylesbury branch continued, but the completion date is uncertain. One source suggests March 1814,[25] which is perfectly feasible assuming the same rate of progress was maintained from the time of Provis' report, but it was reported at the November 1814 meeting of the company that the work was not finished. Soon after this Telford was asked to inspect the branch to answer criticisms about the way it had been built; he reported in May 1815 that it was 'in a very perfect state',[26] and he seemed most impressed with Provis' work. Another factor having a bearing on the opening was Provis' drawings of money from the company to pay for the work. Throughout 1813, when the bulk of the work was being done, Provis was drawing over £1,500 each month, but this dropped steadily in 1814 and finished altogether in June 1815. Another factor was the crucial water supply situation. New reservoirs were built on the Tring summit, specifically to supply the Aylesbury branch, at Tringford and Startopsend. Tringford was started early in 1814 and Startopsend in 1815 and without them, the supply to the main canal would have been very strained. It seems likely that work on the branch was deliberately slowed down in 1814 so that work on the new reservoirs could catch up, with the branch being opened early in 1815 when the water position allowed.

The Western Union project was revived in 1815 when John Rennie made a survey. His plans were approved by the Grand Junction in August 1816, providing the level of the new canal at the Cowley junction was higher than the level of the Grand Junction. Negotiations with the promoters took place in September, but no action resulted. Two years later the Kennet & Avon decided to postpone the project for yet another year. In 1819, however, that company decided to go ahead and in July the Grand Junction again approved the scheme, but with similar safeguards about the water levels at Cowley. The company also insisted on a surcharge on all iron entering its waterway from the new canal to protect the Staffordshire iron trade. A prospectus for the Western Union was issued which showed that the 12 mile long canal, with a branch to Windsor, would cost some £130,000.

Considerable opposition was encountered when the Bill was presented to Parliament, foremost being the Thames Commissioners and the Wilts & Berks Canal Company which had revived its Western Junction plans early in 1818. Telford had surveyed this and the Grand Junction had approved the plans, but with similar compensation tolls to the Western Union. It was obvious there was insufficient trade to justify both canals being built and in May 1820 the Grand Junction decided that both schemes would be to their advantage, but if the Wilts & Berks and Kennet & Avon companies mutually opposed each other, they would probably prevent either scheme being carried out. Despite the opposition, the Western Union Bill passed its second reading in the House of Commons in May 1820, but then the Grand Junction decided to increase the surcharge on iron. The Bill ran into difficulties in the committee stage, largely, it seems, on account of the surcharge, to which Lord Shaftesbury took particular exception. The company would not relent and partly for this reason, but also because of the continuing opposition, the Bill was withdrawn shortly before the end of July. This was virtually the end of the Western Junction and Western Union projects, although both were reconsidered in various forms at odd times in the next few years.

Apart from the major branches several smaller ones were built to connect with the Grand Junction main line. Shortly after 1800 a large fortified depot was built at Weedon in Northamptonshire close to the Grand Junction. The depot was provided as a precaution in case of an invasion by Napoleon, so that the King and Cabinet could retreat to a safe place. A branch canal some five-eighths of a mile in length was opened in April 1804 to serve the depot, a feature of this short branch being the two portcullises under which boats had to pass to gain entry into the fortified part of the depot. These portcullises were raised and lowered by hand-operated machinery housed in the buildings above. The branch was used mainly for the supply of stores, arms and ammunition and also, in the early days when troops were ferried by canal boats, as opposed to the tedious business of marching, the depot was often a port of call for the troops so that they could spend the night there. Later, a branch railway line was built into the depot, but the canal remained in use until about 1920. Most of the branch has been retained as a static water supply but about 300yd at the extreme end has been filled in. The portcullises still guard the entrances to the depot as a reminder of the past and some of the operating machinery survives, although it no longer functions.

A small group of waterways was built in the Rickmansworth area. The first was from the main canal at Batchworth about 500yd up to a wharf in Rickmansworth town. Basically a canalisation of the river Chess through one lock, the branch was constructed by, or for, Salters brewery, which was sited close to the new wharf in the town, and was opened in 1805.[27] In its early days the principal traffic on Salters Cut, as it was known, was barrels to and from Uxbridge. Another branch at Rickmansworth was on the other side of the canal to Batchworth mill. This, about 150yd long, was built by John Dickinson, the mill owner, and opened in August 1818.[28] Just below Batchworth bridge another branch ran just over 300yd in a northerly direction into the Bury Grounds at

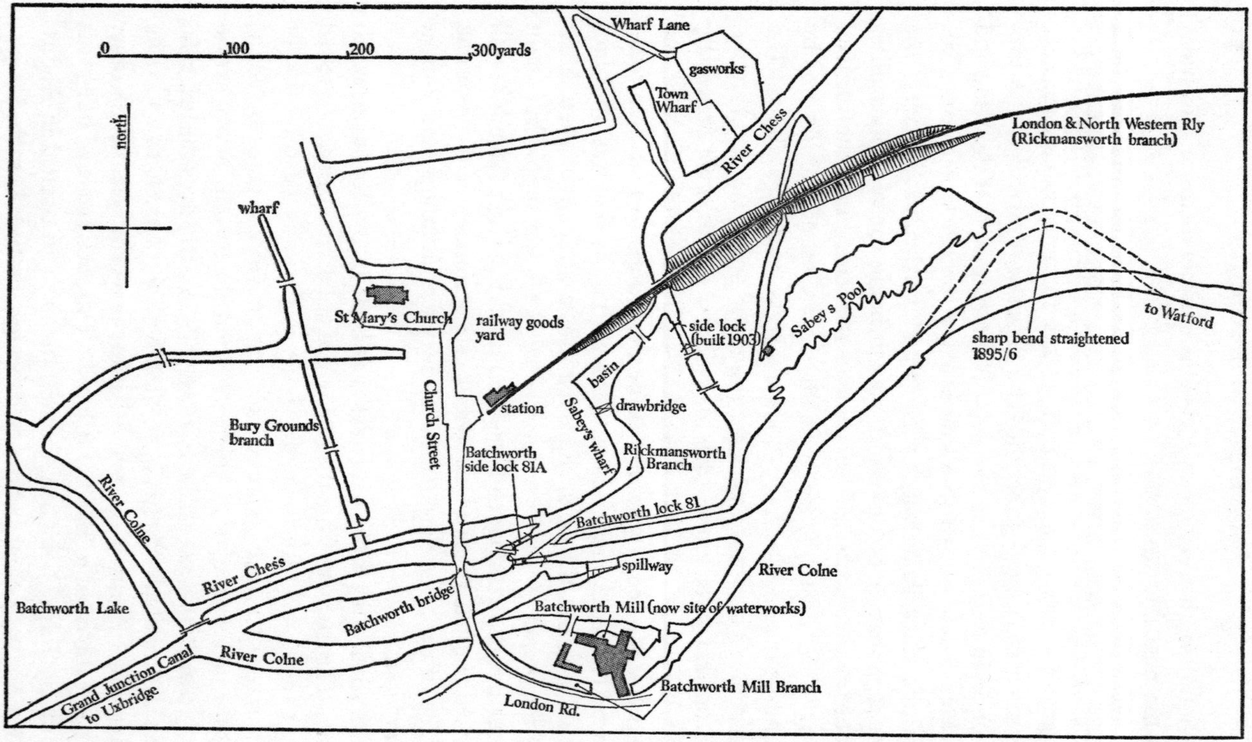

FIGURE 9. Rickmansworth

Rickmansworth. This branch was built for a baker called John Taylor in 1845 to enable flour to be carried up to his bakehouse. Halfway up its course the branch is crossed by a section of the river Chess. Further south another branch was built probably in the 1810s to serve Troy mill at West Hyde and some chalk pits nearby. About half a mile long with no locks, it was certainly open in 1822.

In the London area a whole series of short branches or extended docks was developed. One of the earliest was the short branch of about 300yd to serve the Treaty wharf in Uxbridge, which was opened in the middle of 1798. Just south of Cowley lock Christopher Tower opened the 350yd long Cowley Hall Dock in 1811, whilst at Cowley Peachey a short dock was opened probably in the early 1800s to which the packet boats ran from Paddington. The dock is still known as Packet Boat Dock and nearby stands 'The Paddington Packet Boat' inn on the Uxbridge road. In March 1818 John Mills obtained the company's permission to build a dock at Yiewsley to open up supplies of clay for brickmaking. This dock, known as Otter Dock, was opened in 1820 and after various extensions was eventually over a mile in length. Another dock into a brickfield was opened between 1811 and 1822 near Dawley. This was Pocock's Dock, which after several extensions was nearly five-eighths of a mile long. Later it was operated by Broad & Co, who renamed it Broad's Dock. Near Southall another branch was built to serve the Ordnance Depot there. This followed an approach by the Board of Ordnance in August 1813 and the dock was opened in 1818 to serve the depot at North Hyde. At the end of the 1800s the dock was extended and became known as the Hanwell Military Depot Loop. Many other docks were also built, particularly in the Dawley and Hayes areas, into brickfields to supply the growing London market.

Several other short branches were built on other parts of the canal. At Braunston a branch of just over 200yd was opened, probably in August 1816, to serve a warehouse built by the company alongside the Daventry road. At Stoke Bruerne James Ebbern was allowed to make a short dock of about 50yd in length to the mill by the top lock and this was opened about May 1842, whilst in March 1846 George Savage was allowed to make another dock just over 100yd long into land owned by the Duke of Grafton, for whom Savage was agent. This dock served the Stoke Brick & Tile Works. At Leighton Buzzard a trader called Grant, who had a wharf there, applied to make a dock nearly 50yd long into his premises in December 1800. This was one of the first of many such requests the company was to receive. These were usually granted, as in this case, providing the company's engineer was satisfied and providing an adequate bridge was erected if the towing path were being cut through. Often a nominal rent was charged.

In addition to the branches that were actually built, many others failed to materialise. The Chesham branch was almost certainly intended to follow the course of the river Chess from Rickmansworth. Chesham was a small market town at the time and the considerable expense of building a 9 mile branch rising 150ft can hardly have been justified. The Daventry branch was to have been $1\frac{3}{8}$ miles long, rising 50ft to Daventry through nine locks. Probably it was mainly intended as a water supply branch to the Braunston summit, for the town was hardly big enough to justify a branch otherwise. Later part of the line was taken for the large Daventry reservoir, which removed the need for a branch. The Dunstable branch was planned to run in a straight line from Puddle Hill, just north of Dunstable on Watling Street, to Slapton roughly parallel with the river Ousel. Opposition from the landowners put a stop to the scheme both in 1794 and when it was revived later. As a result Dunstable had to be content with being supplied from a wharf at Bulbourne. The short branch of about 1 mile that was proposed to Hemel Hempstead was intended to follow the course of the river Gade. The town petitioned the company to try and get the branch built but was unsuccessful, for though it had a busy market the company probably felt it was too small, and the main canal came near enough, to warrant the expense of building a branch. Later in the 1840s the idea was revived, but nothing was done.

The Watford branch was intended to follow the course of the river Colne for 2¾ miles as a canalisation of the river. Watford was of sufficient importance to justify the building of this branch, but when the course of the main line was altered to pass much nearer to the town the need for it became less obvious. The Earls of Clarendon and Essex approached the company in 1796 to try and get the branch built, but the company replied in September that work could only start if the people of Watford would advance sufficient funds to finance it. In 1799 the two Earls renewed their appeal, but a vital factor was the restriction on carrying coal southwards on the canal (see Chapter 5) and the company suggested a railway to the town. This idea did not suit their lordships and the matter was dropped.

The lack of action on the Watford branch also affected that to St Albans, which was to have been an extension up the valleys of the Colne and the Ver for about 8 miles. Opposition from landowners had forced the company to spend nearly £3,000 in surveying and parliamentary fees, and to recoup this sum an additional toll of 2d per ton was authorised in the Act for all goods passing on the branch, until the expenses had been repaid. The project for the branch had originated in the autumn of 1792 when Lord Verulam and the Mayor of St Albans had written to Praed about their fears that the town might be left with no outlet to a waterway.[29] Barnes' proposed plan was approved at a public meeting in the town on 26 August and a deputation attended a company meeting to press for the acceptance of the plan. A subscription was opened to defray expenses and John Cowper, an ex-mayor and alderman of the town, was appointed to act on the borough's behalf. It was perhaps the extra toll, which would have deterred traffic, and the continuing opposition of the millers that made the company reluctant to proceed, despite continuing encouragement from Lord Verulam. In July 1808 Praed said the company had no inclination to go ahead and later, in 1816, there was a fresh plan for a railway to take the place of the branch canal. The company decided to support this project, which was to be carried out by a separate company, and to make available the iron rails not now needed for the Northampton railway. In February 1817 it was agreed to subscribe £300 towards the purchase of additional rails that would be needed. But it seems the necessary financial support was not forthcoming from St Albans and the project died. The line was to have run from the main canal at Belswaines, just south of Hemel Hempstead, which was the nearest point on the canal, to St Albans. In 1813 there was a proposal for a canal to Luton, probably from Ivinghoe, but it came to nothing.

In addition to these branches there were several proposals to link the river Great Ouse with the Grand Junction. Early suggestions were for canals from the river Ivel, a navigable tributary of the Ouse, at Shefford to Fenny Stratford and from Bedford to Fenny Stratford by two possible routes. In November 1811 there was a meeting in Bedford to consider a canal to the Grand Junction and Francis Giles carried out a survey, acting under orders from John Rennie. Two possible lines were again suggested; from Bedford to Woughton, north of Fenny Stratford; and from Bedford to Soulbury, south of Fenny. The decision to adopt the Woughton line was taken and a prospectus for the Bedford Canal was issued in July 1812. The line was to be about 15 miles long with twenty-five locks all falling to the Ouse and with nineteen in a flight near Brogborough, where a 1,220yd tunnel was needed. The estimate was £180,807 with tonnage calculated as from 60,000 to 70,000 tons each year with corn from East Anglia passing to Birmingham and Manchester, coal and manufactured goods being received in exchange.[30] There was considerable opposition from local landowners and although the Grand Junction originally put itself down to subscribe £12,000, it later reduced its offer to £3,000. This proved a serious setback, probably caused by a report the company received from Bevan about the state the river Ouse was in at the time. Although about £25,000 was raised locally this was not nearly enough for the scheme to go ahead and the plan fizzled out in 1815. As part of this a suggestion was made for a connection from the Bedford Canal near Marston Moretaine to a proposed London & Cambridge

Junction Canal to open up a direct line to Cambridgeshire and Hertfordshire.

In 1814 there was a proposal to canalise the upper river from Newport Pagnell downstream to Sharnbrook, whence a canal was proposed to link up with the river again at St Neots. Connection with the Grand Junction was to be made by an extension of the Newport Pagnell Canal, then about to be built. Some massive engineering works, coupled with opposition from Bedford, which would have been bypassed, ensured this scheme got nowhere.[31] In 1824 John Rennie and Francis Giles revived the plan for a canal from Shefford to Fenny Stratford, whilst in 1838 and again in 1844 attempts were made to revive the Bedford Canal on a slightly different line, with Giles and Bevan doing surveys, but all without success. A final proposal was made in 1892 for a Bedford & Grand Junction Canal, which proposed a 17 mile canal from Kempston, near Bedford, to Soulbury through twenty-five locks.[32] A company was formed which was to have a capital of £360,000, and be empowered to buy the Ouse navigation from Bedford downstream. It was the proposal for taking over the river that caused much local authority opposition and the Bill was withdrawn in July 1892.

CHAPTER 5

The Early Days

QUITE apart from the numerous engineering problems involved in building the main line and branches and the sheer size of the project, probably the most pressing matter confronting the company in its early days was concerned with finance. The original Act had authorised the raising of £600,000 and, to start with, calls on the shares were made frequently—for instance in September 1793, December 1793, March 1794 and July 1794. It soon became obvious that much more money would have to be raised; this course was decided on in July 1795, and at their half yearly meeting on 3 November the shareholders gave their consent for an application to Parliament for powers to increase the capital. The Act[1] received the Royal Assent on 24 December 1795 and authorised the raising of a further £225,000. In fact 4,500 half shares of £50 each were issued, holders of two half shares being entitled to one vote. The Act also authorised an additional tonnage rate of $\frac{1}{4}$d per ton per mile on lime, limestone, ironstone and other stone, bricks, tiles, slate, coal and manure and an additional $\frac{1}{2}$d per ton per mile on all other goods.

This increased capital soon proved insufficient, particularly as the company was going to have to spend heavily on developing its water supply business in Paddington, and by the Act of 1798 a further £150,000 was authorised. A loan was eventually arranged carrying interest at 5 per cent and convertible into ordinary shares at par in the early 1800s. This became known as the First Optional Loan and £165,000 was raised by this means.[2] In November 1798 as an economy measure it was decided to discontinue the payment of interest on the share capital from 24

Page 103 Paddington: (*above*) a crowded scene in 1909. The entrance to the basin is on the right; (*below*) stop and toll office at Delamere Terrace

Page 104 Watford: (above) Ironbridge lock, Cassiobury Park; (below) wharf at
Cassiobridge

June 1798. Interest was then being paid at 5 per cent and this cost the company no less than £92,404 before the practice was stopped. Instead, and as the tolls for the three years to 29 September 1798 had yielded over £15,000, it was decided that income from June 1798 should be applied towards the payment of dividends. Another economy measure taken a year earlier in September 1797 was to discontinue Jessop's appointment as chief engineer. Instead he was retained as a consultant, but he continued to be just as busy in the company's affairs.

Capital was still short and in the autumn of 1800 it was decided to seek further Parliamentary powers. On 20 June 1801 an Act[3] was passed authorising the raising of another £150,000, bringing the capital up to £1,125,000. Authority was given in the Act for the £100 and £50 shares to be broken down still further to the equivalent number of £12½ shares if required, but this was not carried out. This Act also amended the agreement with the Corporation of London. From the passing of the original Act to 25 December 1798 there was a deficiency of £1,562 in the tolls to the Corporation, which the company had had to make good. It was now agreed that the company would pay £600 each year from 25 December 1798 in lieu of the deficiency payments and the Act transferred to the company the rights to the ½d per ton toll on all craft passing between the Thames and the canal. There were increasing problems in obtaining more capital from the long suffering shareholders and further loans had to be arranged to keep the work going. A Second Optional Loan raised £100,000, a Third £28,000 and a Fourth £80,920, all at 5 per cent and carrying rights to convert into ordinary shares in 1808. In addition nearly £40,000 was raised on mortgages.[4]

By the beginning of 1802 it was obvious that substantially larger sums were still needed and once more the company was fast approaching the limit Parliament had authorised it to raise. Moreover, there was now growing concern and criticism at the canal's seemingly insatiable appetite for funds and the half yearly shareholders meeting in June went into the whole matter with great thoroughness. Of the £1,125,000 authorised by Parliament,

G

£1,104,610 had been raised, although there was still some £60,000 to be paid over to the company. No less than £1,067,023 had been spent on the capital works up to the end of May 1802, whilst £1,039,909 had been received, which included £32,435 from the sale of surplus land. The deficit of £27,104 had been financed partly with a £12,000 loan from the treasurers and partly from the company's ordinary revenue. But there were other capital debts of £74,615 which the company was proposing to pay with the £60,000 still owing and by selling some more land surplus to its requirements, with an estimated value of nearly £15,000.[5]

Meanwhile Barnes produced a long report showing why the works were costing so much more than the estimate. Basically there had been an all round and heavy increase in prices since 1792 when the estimates were made, caused mainly by the outbreak of the Napoleonic wars. A labourer's wage had gone up from 2s per day to 3s 6d (10p–17½p); the price of oak had risen from 1s 8d per foot to 2s 3d (8½p–11p); elm from 10d per foot to 1s 2d (4p–6p); and fir from £3 10s per load to £6 15s (£3.50–£6.75). Similarly in 1793 the hire of a waggon with five horses cost 18s (90p) per day, but the price had almost doubled to £1 15s (£1.75). Quite apart from this, the company's Act had imposed several conditions not allowed for in the estimate. For instance the turf and top 9in of soil had to be removed before spoil banks or back cutting was started and replaced afterwards, whilst in addition the company was compelled to purchase certain odd bits of land the owners no longer wanted as they had been split up by the canal. These two conditions alone cost almost £34,000.

Not only this but the scope of the whole undertaking had grown enormously. Although the original estimate had provided for branches to Daventry and Watford which had not been cut, much longer branches to Buckingham and Paddington had been built instead, whilst the Wendover line had been made navigable at an additional cost of £13,000. Land and rents paid on the Paddington arm alone had cost £11,900, with the wharves and other facilities at Paddington basin amounting to a further £16,000. The rise in the price of labour, estimated at 1d per day for 800 men for eight years, totally £99,840; the increased cost of waggons, horse teams, iron, timber and an additional duty on bricks amounted to almost £44,000; and the price of land had risen on average by £25 per acre, costing £22,500.

In addition, varying the line between Southall and West Drayton, through Cassiobury and Grove parks, and across the Ouse valley had cost £47,000 more than the estimate. Extra reservoirs had been provided costing £14,360 and the whole canal had been made 6in deeper and slightly wider than planned with the locks 6ft longer and 6in deeper, with a view to admitting the same size of boat as was then operating on the river Trent, at a cost of £16,740. The expense of interest paid out on capital, the cost of the wharf at Whitefriars, and dealing with the many unforeseen problems that arose such as at Braunston and Tring completed a long list totalling £640,000 At the time it was thought that £185,000 would be required to complete the canal. To tide matters over the shareholders approved the raising of £20,390, the balance of the outstanding powers, by a loan and also gave their approval for another application to Parliament, the eighth, to authorise the raising of more money. The expenses of the first eight Acts alone had totalled £16,000.

By November, however, a revised estimate of outstanding capital expenditure was presented to the shareholders showing that at least £347,000 was needed. The main items were the tunnel, deep cuttings and locks at Blisworth costing £70,000; the aqueduct and embankment at Wolverton £40,000; pipes and other works in connection with the supply of water to Paddington £55,000; the proposed Boulters lock canal £55,000 and additional reservoirs £22,000. Moreover, land had been acquired that was still not paid for, claims for damage had still to be met; there were other debts, too, and outstanding purchases that would have to be made. Even this was not all, for additional facilities were needed at Paddington which were likely to cost £10,000, whilst if the proposed branch was extended beyond Boulters lock to Reading another £80,000 would be needed, bringing the capital requirements up to almost £440,000.[6]

The new Act[7] received the Royal Assent on 24 March 1803 and authorised the raising of an additional £400,000. Initially it was decided to raise the money by a one for four rights issue to the existing share and loan holders, which should produce £234,500. As much of the money was to be used on Blisworth tunnel and Wolverton aqueduct a toll was authorised in the Act on all goods passing these works. This was 8d per ton through Blisworth and 4d per ton over Wolverton for coal and coke, lime, stones, building materials, ironstone and manure, but double for all other goods. By June 1804 over £200,000 had been raised by the new subscription, whilst at the same time practically all of the First Optional Loan had been converted into shares. The company's capital then stood at £1,328,295 comprising:[8]

	£
Original whole shares of £100 each	465,700
4,500 half shares of £50 each	225,000
First Optional Loan converted	163,887½
New Subscription	208,025
	1,062,612½
Loans (all at 5 per cent interest):	
First Optional Loan unconverted	1,112½
Second Optional Loan	100,000
Third Optional Loan	28,000
Fourth Optional Loan	89,250
Mortgages	47,320
	£1,328,295

Even this was not the end of the saga, for in another Act,[9] the tenth in the company's history, which received the Royal Assent on 27 June 1805 an additional toll of ¼d per ton per mile was authorised on all goods except coal, coke, timber, manure, ashes, bricks and stone, limestone, ironstone and wrought and cast iron. An additional toll of 6d (2½p) per ton on all goods except lime, ashes and manure was also authorised for short haul traffic which passed through any lock on a journey of less than 8 miles. The clause in the first Act under which all government goods had to be carried toll free was amended, as this had become a considerable burden to the company.

Meanwhile receipts were rising. Though the first section of the canal had been opened towards the end of 1794, it was some years before the revenue built up to substantial proportions. Indeed in 1795 a mere £377 was collected, but thereafter the figure increased rapidly as trade became established on the canal and further stretches of waterway were opened. By 1799 the revenue was almost £10,000 and nine years later it was over £100,000; then followed a steady rise to reach a peak figure of £198,086 in 1836. The figures from 1795 to 1836 averaged over three-year periods are as follows:

Year	Toll Receipts £	Year	Toll Receipts £
1795–7	2,916	1816–18	147,537
1798–1800	11,831	1819–21	156,253
1801–3	23,007	1822–4	166,953
1804–6	65,119	1825–7	185,163
1807–9	109,100	1828–30	179,872
1810–12	141,296	1831–3	168,680
1813–15	157,085	1834–6	184,311

In May 1801 it was reported that toll and other income from September 1798 to the end of March 1801 had produced £41,245, with operating expenses for the same period amounting to nearly £28,000, and a dividend of 2 per cent was declared in the form of a credit on the shares until such time as the company could afford to pay over the money. Payment was eventually made at the beginning of February 1803. Receipts up to December 1802 exceeded expenditure by £10,572 and a second dividend of 1½ per cent was declared in February 1803 and paid in April of the same year. The company's share capital then totalled £694,925 and the dividend absorbed £10,424. It was not until 1806 that the payment of dividends settled down to a regular basis. In October 1805 a third dividend of 1 per cent was declared and paid in February 1806, whilst in 1806 two payments of 1½ per cent were declared, one in June and the other in November, to be paid in

August 1806 and January 1807 respectively. Thereafter two payments were made each year except in 1816 when there was exceptionally heavy expenditure on new reservoirs and these payments rose to a peak in 1825 at 13 per cent.

The main traffic in those early days, particularly at the southern end of the canal, was coal, grain, flour and ashes. The figures for the town of Uxbridge in 1799 for traffic to and from the river Thames are fairly representative.[10]

	tons		*tons*
Coals	6,650¾	Bricks & Tiles	131½
Grain	4,968½	Stone	108
Flour	4,612½	Coke	68¼
Sundries	1,821½	Loam	49½
Ashes	1,318¼	Timber	18
Manure	164	Lime	14¾
			19,925½

Coal at the southern end of the canal was, at least in the early years, 'Sea Coal', so called because it was shipped by sea from north-east coast ports to London. As early as 1667 this coal had been subjected to a toll by the Corporation of London to enable some of the damage wrought by the Great Fire of 1666 to be repaired. Later, the money raised by the coal dues was used for carrying out improvements in London, such as the Victoria and Albert Embankments. The appearance of the Grand Junction posed a very real threat to the established sea coal trade, for the canal was to have excellent connections with collieries in Warwickshire, Leicestershire and Nottinghamshire. As a result of opposition from the shipping interests a clause in the company's original Act prohibited the carriage of coal any further southwards on the canal than the entrance to the proposed Langleybury tunnel. This spot had to be amended to the north-east end of Grove park, when the new deviated canal line was authorised.

In 1805 this total restriction on coal was eased and 50,000 tons were allowed to pass to Paddington upon payment of the coal

Grand Junction Canal.

We James Palmer and Richard Greene of the City of Lichfield Bankers, Survivors in a joint Account with Robert Scott of the same place Banker deceased

in Consideration of the Sum of *One hundred and fifty five Pounds ten shillings*

paid to **us** by *Robert Watts of Dunstable in the County of Bedford Gentleman* do hereby bargain, sell, assign, and transfer to the said

Robert Watts. One half ———— Share of the Navigation called **The Grand Junction Canal**, being Number *3938. of the half* ————

———— Shares in the said Navigation, **To hold** to the said *Robert Watts his*

Executors, Administrators, and Assigns, subject to the same Rules, Orders, and Restrictions, and on the same Conditions that *he* held the same immediately before the Execution hereof:

And. *I* the said *Robert Watts* ————

do hereby agree to take and accept the said *One half* ————

———— Share subject to the said Rules, Orders, Restrictions, and Conditions, **As witness** our Hands and Seals the *fifth* ———— Day of *December* in the Year of our Lord One Thousand Eight Hundred and Twenty *seven*

Signed, sealed, and delivered by the said *James Palmer and Richard Greene in the presence of us*   *J. Palmer (L.S.)*

W. Lawton, Lichfield Gent
W. Bickley   do   do   *Rd. Greene (L.S.)*

Signed Sealed and delivered by the said Robert Watts in the presence of us —   *Robt. Watts. (L.S.)*
John Henry Watts of Dunstable, Gentleman
John Sharland of Leighton Buzzard. Accountant

FIGURE 10. A share transfer of 1826

dues. A collector was stationed at Grove to take the dues and keep a record of the tonnage past this point. Later still even this restriction was abolished and any amount of coal was allowed to pass on the canal subject to the payment of the dues. In 1831 these dues were standardised at 1s 1d ($5\frac{1}{2}$p) per ton. One effect of the provisions of the Coal Duties Acts was the setting up of a thriving coal wharf, called Lady Capel's wharf, at Grove, where the restriction applied. With the prohibition on coal passing further southwards on the canal the obvious solution was to offload the coal on to carts, and a substantial trade was built up serving Watford and the immediate district round about. For many years the company operated this wharf under lease from the Earl of Clarendon, but gave it up in 1847 when its tenant left. But even with these restrictions the coal tonnages on the Grand Junction were soon substantial. In 1805 26,700 tons of sea coal and 94,730 tons of inland coal were carried and by 1830 these figures had grown to 39,800 and 149,000 tons respectively.

The early days of the canal were not solely tied up with financial problems. One of the first snags occurred at Fenny Stratford. It is usually assumed that Fenny Stratford lock, which has the smallest lift of any of the Grand Junction system—a mere 12in— was the result of a mistake in the levels, but this is not the case. Between Fenny and Wolverton the canal could not be made to hold water properly; Jessop attributed the trouble to the very rocky ground through which the canal had been cut and the lack of suitable material to line the bed of the waterway. The worst place was a 2 mile stretch just north of Fenny where it was proving virtually impossible to maintain the water level high enough for fully loaded boats.[11] Matters became so bad that the canal had to be closed at this point in May 1802 for repairs to be carried out. To get over the difficulty and purely as a temporary measure a lock was built at Fenny and the level of the entire $11\frac{1}{2}$ mile pound to the top lock of the flight down into the Ouse valley at Wolverton was lowered by about 1ft[12] to below the point where most of the leaks were occurring. The operation was carried out early in June 1802 and it was hoped that the problem could be cured and the level restored to its full height, thus making the lock at Fenny unnecessary.

In the years that followed the company did consider doing away with the lock, but in October 1805, following a report and an estimate of the cost it was decided that the lock should remain, because of the considerable expense of removing it and the delays to traffic whilst the work was being carried out. The matter was reconsidered in 1838 when a scheme to raise the long Fenny pound by 6in and to deepen the 3 mile pound southwards to Stoke Hammond by 6in was examined. But the sheer expense deterred any action being taken and the lock remains today as a permanent part of the Grand Junction scene.

Another problem arose in the Hemel Hempstead area. When planning the canal Jessop and Barnes could little have realised what troubles they would be letting the company in for with the millers by linking up the canal with the rivers Gade and Bulbourne. For as it descends from the Tring summit the canal runs parallel with the river Bulbourne for part of its course. At Winkwell the river and canal unite for a short distance and then divide again— the river to flow through the Boxmoor watercress beds, to pass under the canal near the Fishery Inn through a three-arched culvert and eventually to flow into the river Gade just above Two Waters mill—whilst the canal passes down through the Boxmoor locks to Hemel Hempstead. Meanwhile the river Gade, which rises to the north-west of Great Gaddesden, crosses the canal on the level at a right-angled junction just a short distance from its confluence with the Bulbourne. The canal below Hemel was thus in a position to be fed by the waters of both rivers and this is what caused the trouble.

Downstream from the junction with the Gade the canal used to run for over $1\frac{1}{2}$ miles without a lock—the 'long pound' as it was known—and then there were four locks close together to lower the canal some 28ft down to the level of the Kings Langley pound. This arrangement was bitterly criticised by the owners of Apsley and Nash mills, who contended that much of the water of the two rivers was being diverted to supply the long pound and

(a)

(b)

(c)

(d)

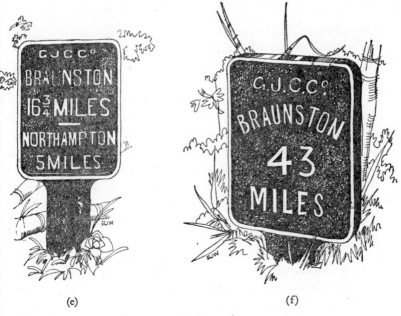

(e)   (f)

FIGURE 11.   Markers and stones

(a) and (b) London coal duties markers; (c) and (d) original milestones; (e) and
(f) 1893 cast-iron mileposts

the flight of locks, rather than their mills. So strong were the
protests that in July 1805 the company decided to erect a steam
engine which would be able to pump water from the bottom of
the four locks back up to the long pound. The engine, which was
supplied by Boulton & Watt of Birmingham, was duly put into
service on a site not far from Nash mill. Amongst the leaders of
the millers was George Stafford of Apsley mill and in February
1807 he put in a claim against the company for nearly £124 for
deficiency of work at his mill because of the diversion of part of
the water supplies between June and December 1805.

A new character appeared on the scene in May 1809 when John
Dickinson purchased Apsley mill from George Stafford.[13] Nearly
two years later, early in 1811, he bought Nash mill as well.
Dickinson had a partner, George Longman, who provided much
of the finance in the early days, the firm trading as Longman &

Dickinson. Both Apsley and Nash were very old mills, which had been mentioned in Domesday Book as corn mills but had both been converted to paper making towards the end of the eighteenth century.[14]

The steam engine at Nash did not solve the problem and in August 1811 Dickinson wrote to the company saying he would commute all his claims against it for £12,000. These claims were investigated and in September it was decided to open negotiations for the company to pay a fixed sum in compensation for the next three years instead of working the steam engine. The annual cost of working and maintaining it was averaging out at £500, which the company thought much too high. It seemed that the long pound was causing most of the trouble because it was not watertight; Bevan thought these leaks could be cured in a few years, after which the steam engine would not be needed. Negotiations with Dickinson were started but they failed to produce an agreement and in July 1812 Longman & Dickinson sued the company for damages. The action was heard before the Master of the Rolls and whilst the millers' claim was not allowed, the Court appear to have upheld many of their grievances and a decree was issued which, amongst other things, ordered the company to prevent any unnecessary waste of water in the long pound.

In February 1813 Dickinson approached the company with new proposals. Firstly he suggested that a new steam engine large enough to replace all the water being drawn from the rivers by the canal should be erected and worked by the company. Alternatively he suggested that the existing engine should be made over to him and the company should supply enough coal to keep it working seven months in a year and to offset labour costs and maintenance. These proposals were referred to Bevan but were rejected in May as being quite unacceptable.

Negotiations again having failed the millers brought another action claiming £4,463 damages for water diverted between May 1814 and January 1815. A sub-committee was appointed to deal with the situation and Thomas Telford was called in to investigate and advise the company. Telford carried out a series of tests, the millers being invited to attend but refusing, and his conclusion at the end of a three-day investigation was that the steam engine more than compensated for any water diverted from the rivers by navigation, the differing capacity of the locks, leakage and other causes alleged by the millers. Meanwhile, a few days before, the millers' engineer Donkin had also been conducting tests and he considered his results proved that the canal was diverting water from the rivers, despite the steam engine. Indeed the amount diverted was said to be no less than one-fifth of the total flow of the rivers, even after allowing for the water returned by the engine.

The action brought by the millers was heard at Hertfordshire Assizes on 3 March before a special jury and the question of damages was referred to Mr Sergeant Bosanquet with power for him to make further investigations during the summer. The company then decided that it would ease the situation considerably to build side ponds at the four locks to cut down their consumption of water and Bevan was told to start work on them in July. There was some trouble in obtaining the land needed, which was owned by Dickinson who was not disposed to be co-operative, but the company was within its Parliamentary powers and strong measures were ordered to prevent any further interference. The side ponds were duly constructed and brought into service, but for the millers the company's action was looked on as not at all the proper solution to their dispute. Indeed it had always been a particular bone of contention that the company had never built the reservoir that was stipulated in the original Act to supply the mills on the Gade and Bulbourne.

The dispute lingered on and in February 1816 the company decided that judgement by default should be suffered so that the whole matter could be tried before the sheriff. In June 1816 the millers brought another action, which the company decided to defend, but the state of war between the two parties could not continue indefinitely and in January 1817 the first steps were taken towards trying to work out an amicable settlement. In February Dickinson produced new proposals to solve the dispute and end the litigation. A meeting was held in April following which Bevan was asked to report on the costs of puddling and maintaining the long pound, maintaining the four locks, operating and maintaining the steam engine for the last three years, and operating and maintaining the side ponds since their construction. Meanwhile Telford was asked to survey the line of a proposed deviation for the canal as suggested by Dickinson and to report generally on this proposal. Telford was also asked to investigate whether the steam engine and the side ponds between them would be sufficient to protect the company against any further claims for damages by the millers, once the long pound had been made watertight.

Telford, with W. A. Provis as assistant, made a survey and the company decided to adopt the idea of a deviated canal as the best way of settling the disputes with the millers.[15] The terms of an agreement were then worked out with Longman & Dickinson and an Act was prepared for submission to Parliament, whilst in December 1817 negotiations were opened with landowners for the purchase of the land needed. The Act[16] received the Royal Assent on 17 March 1818 and authorised the abandonment of the canal from Frogmoor swing bridge to the junction with the tail water of Nash mill and the carrying of the new line into the course of the river Gade. The company was empowered to borrow £30,000 for the work.

Much of the actual brickwork on the new locks required on the diversion was carried out by Dickinson under contract, although in fact he subcontracted some of the work. Operations must have got under way quickly for early in August Dickinson was paid £3,000 on account of work already carried out. By February 1819 the work was nearly complete and the diversion was opened soon afterwards. The total of Dickinson's contract was £10,580, which included £600 for the old bricks, and this was somewhat less than Telford's estimate of £12,000. The actual earthworks were carried out by the company.

The new line of canal went a long way to settling the dispute with the millers, particularly as five new locks of lesser fall and hence using less water were provided to replace the four old locks. As a result, and to avoid renumbering all the locks southwards, lock 69 at Kings Langley was renumbered 69A. In fact the water problem at Apsley and Nash mills was eased somewhat soon afterwards when both were converted to steam-working, the coal being supplied by canal, but considerable amounts of water were still needed for the paper-making process. In 1826 Dickinson opened the new Home Park mill, just over a mile downstream from Nash, and in 1830 Croxley mill south of Watford was opened.[17] Both depended on water power in their early days.

Hemel Hempstead was not the only place where there were disputes with millers. Indeed there were almost inevitably problems whenever the company needed to alter water levels to improve conditions for navigation, with repercussions from mills both up and downstream. At Rickmansworth there was a protracted problem with the level at Strutts Batchworth mill. Barnes made a long report in 1802 about raising the level slightly but the dispute was still going on in March 1809 when the owners offered to sell at a fair price. In June £17,000 was being asked against a company offer of £13,500. By December the company had increased its offer to £16,000 and eventually a price was agreed. But even then it was not until May 1823 that an agreement was reached with the principal landowner and the water level from Lot Mead to Batchworth mill was finally fixed.[18] One reason for the extremely long time taken before an agreement could be reached was because this particular stretch of canal was a vital one in that both rivers Gade and Colne joined it, which meant that many complicated factors had to be taken into account.

Obviously the canal was a mixed blessing to the millers, for whilst they welcomed the advantages of cheap transport, more often their main concern was to ensure that their water supplies were in no way interfered with. In the original Act several clauses were inserted to protect millers, including one that the company was obliged to build a reservoir to supply water to the river Colne to compensate for any river water diverted into the canal.

This reservoir was to be supplied with flood water and the millers on the Colne insisted that the company could only take water from the river if it could be made good from the reservoir. To ensure the company abided by these conditions the millers were empowered to appoint a superintendent at the reservoir, although the company had to pay his salary.

A site for this reservoir was selected at Aldenham and it was one of the earlier works to be started. Indeed it seems the work had probably been completed in November 1795 when parts of it had to be fenced as they were dangerous to local people. The purchase of the land required raised the question of how the money was to be divided between the lord of the manor at Aldenham and others interested in the land. For the land was part of Aldenham common, just over 68 acres being involved, for which the company had agreed to pay £30 per acre. Part of the company's sixth Act, passed in December 1795, set out the procedure for settling the matter, and the company was also given an option to purchase a further ten acres at the same price, which had to be taken up by the following December. It seems that the option was exercised, as in November 1801 Barnes was told to set out the land for an extension to the reservoir not exceeding ten acres. In April 1802 he was also told to arrange a contract for strengthening and raising the headbank at a cost of some £400, probably in connection with this enlargement. Aldenham reservoir is fed by several small streams particularly in the Brockley Hill area to the south. The outlet was down a natural stream into the Colne near Radlett.

It seems that the reservoir gave a fair amount of trouble to start with as slips were continually occurring in the headbank. Jessop made a full report in December 1802 which pinpointed the trouble to the treacherous nature of the clay. This tended to crack in dry weather and he recommended covering it with a protective layer of sand and gravel about 9in thick. Repairs had started on restoring the clay, it being trodden in by horses as Jessop had rejected puddling the clay as totally wrong for this purpose. The gravelling was to follow and finally a thin covering

Page 121   Wolverton aqueduct in 1921: (*above*) refacing work; (*below*) the empty trough

Page 122 (above) Former double bridge and entrance to double lock, Stoke Bruerne, 1907; (below) slab walling at Mountmill, Buckingham branch, 1919

of soil would be added on the outside slope, sown with rye grass. But even these remedial measures were not entirely satisfactory, for in December 1804 the water had to be lowered in a hurry to enable urgent repairs to be carried out. Meanwhile, earlier, in December 1802, Holland had proposed that Aldenham should be enlarged again to hold 1,500 extra locks[19] of water. The cost would be £4,218 and another 21 acres would be needed. Jessop reported against this scheme and recommended raising the head-bank if more water was needed, as this could be done for a third of the cost of the extension. At this time the company was actively looking into other sources of water and no action was taken at Aldenham. Indeed, to combat the recurring troubles with slipping in the headbank, it seems that the water level was actually dropped not long after.

The need for more water in the early 1800s at the southern end of the canal was mainly due to the growth of the Paddington water supply side of the concern, which necessitated an improved supply to the 'Long Level', the pound running from Cowley to Paddington. The most obvious source, the river Colne, could not be used and the same applied to Aldenham reservoir, so a fresh source was urgently needed. One scheme put forward was for a completely new reservoir at Ruislip. A plan had been prepared by Gream early in 1800 and in April of that year the company opened negotiations for the land required. But little can have been done and it was not until October 1803 that Barker was told to resume these purchases. At the time Ruislip common was in the process of being enclosed and in June 1804 the company applied for land to be allocated for a reservoir. The common land was obtained but other land proved harder to obtain. Barker had valued some at £50 an acre but the owners asked £70, and after some haggling the company agreed to £55 in March 1805. The owners of some woodland wanted £65 against Barker's valuation of £25 and this case went to arbitration, with a price eventually being agreed in February 1806. But worst of all was another owner who refused to negotiate at all on any terms. Fortunately, in August 1807 it was reported that the reluctant owner had sold out and the new

H

owner was willing to bargain. But there were still problems, as the owners of two cottages insisted that new cottages should be built in exchange and the company had to agree. At last all the land was obtained and the reservoir was built and put into service. The original outlet followed a natural stream course and entered the canal not far from Norwood top lock. Later part of this feeder was made navigable and became known as Passmore's Dock. But the line gave rise to complaints from the millers on the Colne and to meet their objections in December 1815 it was decided to build an entirely new and shorter feeder to the Paddington branch.

Even with Ruislip in service supplies to the Long Level were still inadequate, besides which the position of Aldenham was unsatisfactory as far as the company was concerned, whilst the millers were unhappy about possible abuses with the company taking water from the Colne. The Duke of Northumberland, who owned many of the mills on the Colne downstream from Uxbridge, was particularly concerned lest water from the river should be diverted to supply the Paddington waterworks. The canal and the river had several junctions north of Uxbridge and it would have been a simple matter for the company to feed river water through Cowley lock to the Long Level. In fact the company was prohibited from doing this by its first Act, but to safeguard the Duke's interests and those of his miller tenants on the Colne another Act[20] was passed on 9 June 1812. By this the company was prohibited from making any new junctions with the river Colne, unless they were already in existence in June 1811. To protect their interests the millers were empowered to appoint a person at both Cowley and Cowroast locks to control the water passing to the Long Level. A special new connection was provided at Cowley lock to link the canal with the Colne and records had to be kept of the destination of all craft which determined whether the lockage water at Cowley was passed to the Long Level or to the Colne through the new connection.

If a boat was passing through Cowley lock to, or from, anywhere short of the Tring summit at Cowroast its lockage water could not be supplied from the summit but would have been drawn from the Colne or one of its tributaries and hence the lockage water had to be returned to the river at Cowley to make good the abstraction. If, however, the boat either went as far as, or came from, the summit the water lost to the Colne was made good from the summit and this lockage water could be passed to the Long Level. The company was also entitled to lockage water for boats passing through Cowroast to or from a destination north of Cowley. The Act also amended the restrictions on Alden-ham reservoir and laid down that the company had to supply the Colne with 320 locks of water between 1 June and 1 November each year from the reservoir as a soakage and evaporation allow-ance. Gauges were provided at various places to determine the quantities of water passing these points. But any excess over and above the special allowance could be passed down to the Long Level and used to supply this section of the canal. This operation was carried out under the strict supervision of the millers' repre-sentatives both at Aldenham and at Cowley, but for the company it was a great improvement on the previous state of affairs in that Aldenham reservoir could now be used to the full.

For many years there were, in effect, two lock-keepers at both Cowley and Cowroast, both paid by the company, but one acting for the company and one for the Duke of Northumberland. In time, with the decline in the number of mills on the Colne and their reliance on water power, the duties of the two supervisors were assumed by the company's keepers, with the Cowroast keeper reporting to his colleague at Cowley the appropriate numbers.

Another source of water investigated by the company was from the river Brent. In June 1803 Barnes reported on a possible site for a reservoir and Jessop was asked to comment. He agreed with the idea and Barker was told to draw up a plan and estimate of the land needed for the work. But in October 1803 the project was deferred. So pressing was the water situation at the time that in April of the following year the Brent was again considered and Jessop was asked to report on a proposal for a feeder from the river at Kingsbury to run to the Paddington branch at Lower Place. Again action was deferred but in 1809 the scheme was revived; Henry Provis carrying out a survey which differed little from the 1804 plan. The feeder was to be 3¼ miles long from Kingsbury through Willesden to Lower Place and having delayed so long the company now decided to go ahead at once and negotiations were opened for the land required. The works were not heavy and the feeder was soon in service. Later the feeder was incorporated into the Brent reservoir scheme which was carried out in the 1830s by the Regent's Canal company, the reservoir being opened in June 1835 and most of the feeder being used for the outlet for the reservoir.

Finding new supplies of water was not the only concern of the company at the time. It also did its best to conserve existing supplies, and as early as December 1803 two experimental side ponds were built at locks 58 and 59 just south of Berkhamsted. In April 1805 Bevan issued a report on the extra time needed to work through these locks and on the costs of construction and it was then decided to install side ponds at several other locks to conserve water supplies at key points. An obvious place was at Norwood and Hanwell, where locks carried the canal down from the Long Level to the lower reaches of the river Brent and where any saving would relieve pressure on the supplies to Paddington. For some reason construction was deferred and it was not until 1815 that a contract was given to John Woodhouse for building the eight side ponds needed. In December Provis reported that Woodhouse's work was so bad that the side ponds were unusable. Woodhouse carried out repairs but Provis was still complaining in May 1816 that leaks on the Hanwell flight had been caused by rubbish from the work being thrown into the canal and preventing the gates and paddles from closing properly.

At Brentford there was another problem with the millers. Originally there was no lock downstream from Brentford lock No 100 and Brentford bridge, the river Brent being tidal to this point. In fact boats could only pass for limited periods at high tide and in September 1802 a series of complaints from canal users was received about the perpetual delays and general inconvenience of navigating this section. The users suggested either widening and deepening the river or cutting a new channel southwards into the deep waters of the Thames. To try and prolong the brief period of time navigation was possible the company had erected flood gates, which held up the level for a while after the tide had turned, but this brought complaints from Richard Kidd, whose mill was on this part of the river, about the water backing up to his mill and preventing his wheel from working properly. Kidd asked either for an allowance towards the cost of altering his wheel and a £100 annuity for the privilege of holding up the water, or that his whole interest should be bought out for £2,000. William Jackson was told to negotiate with Kidd and to offer no more than £1,750 for the mill. Jackson must have been a good negotiator for he got the mill for £1,500.

The obvious course would have been to build a lock at the entrance to the canal in the first place, but the company's Act specified that the free navigation of the Brent was not to be impeded in any way. Despite this, once the company owned the mill rights, it was probably an easy matter to convince landowners and others that it would be in everyone's best interests to have a proper lock, and Thames lock was soon in service in place of the flood gates. Eventually in 1818 the mill was demolished and a set of flood gates erected in place of the old mill sluices.

Once the main line of the canal was complete the problems confronting the company tended to diminish in some ways, but there were still many other matters to attend to. As traffic built up so it became necessary to appoint a number of toll clerks to collect the tonnage dues at various key points. The first two were stationed at Brentford and Uxbridge and another was appointed at Braunston in 1796. By January 1802 there were eleven in the company's employment, the senior and highest paid being James Cherry, the first of a long line of Cherrys in the service of the Grand Junction, at Braunston with a salary of £90 per annum, showing that this was already the most important toll station on the whole canal. The clerk at Brentford received £85,

Paddington £80, Blisworth £75, Stoke Bruerne £70, Wendover junction, Marsworth £60, Buckingham junction, Cosgrove £55 and Boxmoor, Bulls Bridge, Great Linford and Harefield all £50 each. Soon afterwards an assistant was appointed at Braunston to help James Cherry and in September 1808 another, indicating Braunston's continuing role as the leading toll station.

As trade developed and new sections of waterway were opened changes were made to the toll stations. For instance, when Blisworth tunnel was completed the station at Stoke was probably closed and when the Northampton branch was opened the Blisworth office was moved to the junction. Similarly when the Grand Union Canal was opened a station was established at Long Buckby, whilst in 1818 an office was opened at Fenny Stratford, although this seems to have had a short life and was soon moved to Leighton Buzzard. Under the company's Act all boats were supposed to have graduated metal scales fixed on the side so that their loading could be determined. But to assist the toll clerks the company decided in August 1799 that all boats were to be gauged and their displacement recorded for known loadings. These records were kept at all the toll stations and the toll clerks, by measuring displacement, could easily calculate the tonnage from the gauging table. The gauging of boats was started by the company in the early 1800s and soon became standard throughout the Grand Junction system.

In June 1805 the company's engineer James Barnes retired after a magnificent thirteen years of service. He had dedicated himself to the Grand Junction and the opening of the main canal represented his crowning achievement. Even in retirement he was not far away as he lived at Braunston. In June 1803 the canal had been divided for administrative purposes into three districts. Initially these were the Northern district from Braunston to Leighton Buzzard, which district included most of the major engineering works; the Middle district from Leighton to Hunton Bridge and the Southern district from Hunton Bridge to Brentford and Paddington. John Woodhouse was appointed engineer of the Northern district in September 1805; he was succeeded after a few years by William Thompson, who remained until his retirement in 1835. When Barnes retired Benjamin Bevan and Henry Provis looked after the Middle and Southern districts on an informal basis, but Bevan left the company at the end of April 1817 and Thomas Lake was then appointed engineer to the Middle district. Provis left in 1816, Richard Trubshaw being appointed engineer to the Southern district in November 1816. Dismissed in December 1821, his place was taken by John Holland.

In the early years the company's finances were looked after by Philip Box, a banker at Buckingham, but in November 1801 he reported that he had entered into a new partnership with William Praed, the company's chairman, and in November Box and Praed were appointed joint treasurers. In the early days the company often had to rely on the help of its treasurers and in November 1802 it was decided that the company's two offices at Fludyer Street and Winchester Row, Paddington should be amalgamated as near to the treasurer's office in Fleet Street as possible. In January 1803 the offices were transferred to Essex Street, Strand, but in 1805 the office moved to its final resting place at 21 Surrey Street, Strand. Meanwhile in October 1805 Acton Chaplin and Edward Gray resigned as clerks to the company and Charles Harvey, who had been appointed superintendent in June 1805, temporarily stepped into the breach. On 5 November 1805 Richard Cowlishaw Sale, the committee clerk, was appointed clerk, with Harvey becoming secretary. In March 1816 Charles Simpson of Lichfield replaced Harvey, but Simpson died in December 1820 and in the following year it was decided to discontinue the secretary's office and instead have a full-time chairman and clerk. William Praed now stepped down after a wonderful record of service of nearly thirty years and the Hon Philip Pleydell Bouverie was appointed chairman in his place on 9 February 1821. From the same day Sale assumed the position of full-time clerk.

There were many smaller problems. For instance in April 1811 the Earl of Clarendon objected to boats using the canal on Sundays. Trying to be helpful, the company instructed its lock-keepers to stop boats passing during the hours of church service, but this upset the Earl of Essex, who was afraid of what the boatmen might get up to during this period of enforced idleness. It was all very trying, and to relieve its feelings the company donated one hundred guineas to the relief of some Portuguese sufferers. In 1816, following a decision at the half yearly general assembly, it was decided to set up a Select Committee to relieve the general committee of much routine work. The select committee was a smaller and more streamlined body, with a maximum of nine members. Praed was the chairman with Thomas Cobb as his deputy and the first meeting was on 11 June 1816. The first resolution was that a clock should be bought for the committee room; thereafter they met at frequent intervals and carried out much of the ordinary day to day business that would otherwise have gone to the full general committee for a decision.

Another early matter to be dealt with by the select committee was the debt due to the company from Pickfords, one of the main carrying concerns on the canal. Pickfords enjoyed generous credit terms from the company, but even then they trespassed somewhat on this hospitality. At the beginning of September 1816 £4,473 was owing in respect of May's tonnage and rent due, and Pickfords were written to. There had been no response by the end of the month and an ultimatum was issued saying that unless £2,000 was paid by 2 October their credit was to be stopped at Paddington. These threats brought Mr Parke of Pickfords to a meeting at the end of October, by which time the July tonnages of £2,298 were nearly due. Parke pleaded that the suspension should not be brought into effect and promised prompter payment in future. His diplomacy succeeded but this was not the last time that Pickfords' debt caused the company some concern.

Nevertheless the financial position had improved very considerably from the early 1800s, when affairs had been decidedly strained. In 1803 a sinking fund was set up, which by October 1808 amounted to £70,000.[21] Indeed in October 1817 the fund was in such a healthy state that it was decided to repay the various loan stocks, the Aylesbury canal subscription and a debt due to the Trustees of Dr Radcliffe for land at Wolverton, especially as exchequer bills, in which most of the money was invested, bore interest at a mere 3 per cent. In January 1818 Sale gave formal notice to pay off all the mortgages and loans next September, when interest on them would stop. Those holding over £200 could hold a new loan stock carrying interest at 4 per cent, a reduction of 1 per cent. The only other loan issued since 1802 was a Fifth Optional Loan. This was launched on 2 November 1804 and had collected £75,513 by March 1806. At the time of the loans repayment in 1818 the issued ordinary share capital stood at £1,181,550, at which figure it remained until 1820 when a gradual reduction started, which by 1846 had reached £1,145,500. And so in this healthy state the company moved into the Railway Age to face by far its biggest problems.

CHAPTER 6

Tring and Braunston Summits

A MAJOR problem that confronted the Grand Junction, in common with most other canal managements, was that of providing an adequate water supply to the summit levels. Both the Grand Junction's summits had their own particular difficulties, but those at Tring always seemed to be more acute than those at Braunston.

A few very small streams were encountered on the 3 mile Tring summit itself, but these were of only minor significance. The main supply has always been obtained from the Wendover feeder branch, which joins the main line at the north end of the summit just above lock 45. The feeder runs along the north side of the Chilterns and on its course to Wendover intercepts several streams. These occur at the junction of the various strata of which the hills are made up—a water-bearing chalk, lying on a thin layer of Totternhoe stone, which in turn lies on an impervious chalk marl.

The first stream tapped is the Tring feeder, which enters just above New Mill. Originally this was fed by the surplus water not required to operate the mill, but after the mill was purchased by the company it went out of use and the entire supply, which varies from about 8 to 25 locks per day, now enters the canal.[1] The next stream taken is about half a mile from the Wendover end of the branch. In 1848 nearly £2,000 was spent on culverting it and driving a heading into the nearby hillside to increase the yield. Now this source, called the 'heading', yields from 2 to 10 locks per day. But the main source of water, which enters at the extreme end of the branch, is the Wendover stream. This formerly ran into the river Thame and it provides from 4 to 20 locks per day.[2]

To compensate millers at Aylesbury for the water of this stream diverted into the canal at Wendover a reservoir was built at Weston Turville in 1797 and 1798, a short distance from the branch. The reservoir was fed by two small streams and, in winter, by surplus water from the feeder. Later the company purchased the milling rights and the practice of supplying compensation water was discontinued. Indeed in 1814, when the demand for water was particularly pressing, a well and heading were built so that water from Weston Turville could be pumped into the branch. This was intended as a temporary measure but, in fact, the steam engine installed remained in use for nearly twenty-five years. After that the reservoir was virtually abandoned for many years with the water level being kept down.

Once the canal was opened over Tring summit it was realised that in summer water supplies were barely adequate. This was spotlighted during a drought in the early 1800s. To ease the problem, construction of a new reservoir was started in 1802 on low-lying ground near Wilstone to the north of the Wendover feeder. It was fed by two small springs, the Ashwell Head and the Barwell Head, and by a stream from Drayton Beauchamp, the Drayton feeder. Arrangements were made to run surplus water off the summit to the new reservoir by means of some paddles at Drayton, which connected with the Drayton feeder. To pump water from Wilstone into the summit a well was sunk beside the Wendover branch at Whitehouses and an underground tunnel, or heading, was built to the reservoir. A pump of 30 locks per day capacity was installed at Whitehouses with a steam engine to drive it. Considerable difficulties were encountered, which delayed progress, particularly in the heading where large quantities of water were tapped and it was not until June 1803 that the task was completed.[3]

Meanwhile in the spring of 1802 a loss of water by leakage through the banks of the Wendover branch had been noticed. Temporary repairs were made but in the autumn of 1803 the branch from Whitehouses to the main line had to be closed for more comprehensive action to be taken. It was not reopened until the early summer of 1804, and even then the work was not completed. During the closure all the Wendover water was run down into Wilstone reservoir until it was full and then to waste. Benjamin Bevan, who had been placed in charge of the repair work in March 1804, submitted a scheme for a new reservoir to be used for storing this surplus water from the summit. His proposal was adopted in December 1805 and the reservoir built in 1806 between the Wendover branch and the Marsworth flight of locks. This reservoir is connected to the main canal by a paddle above lock 41 and a weir above lock 40 so that it can be supplied from the summit by running water down the locks. There is also an independent supply from the Bulbourne feeder, a spring which rises near the company's Bulbourne workshops. This has now been culverted throughout its length, passing under the main canal and the Wendover branch on its way, and it yields from 1 to 7 locks per day. Marsworth reservoir, as the new reservoir was called, was intended to supply water to the canal north of the summit and water can be discharged by paddles into the canal above and below lock 39. In 1810 a well was sunk alongside the Wendover branch not far from the junction with the main line, a steam pump was set up and a heading driven to enable water from Marsworth reservoir to be pumped direct to the summit in times of shortage. But after 1817, when Startopsend reservoir was opened, the engine was dismantled, as surplus water from Marsworth could be run into Startopsend. The pumping shaft and heading were then used for running surplus water from the summit to the reservoir.

In its 1812 Act the company was empowered to construct an additional reservoir on the Tring summit to supply the Aylesbury branch canal, construction of which was about to begin, but the Act did allow the company to supply this water by way of the summit if required. In fact two reservoirs were built. The first, a high level one named Tringford, was begun in April 1814 and completed in 1816, and the other, Startopsend, alongside the existing Marsworth reservoir, in 1815 and finished in 1817. Tringford is fed by the Tring Drainage, which passes under the

Wendover branch in a culvert, and is supplied also by surface drainage from various parts of Tring.[4] Before New Mill was purchased by the company the water, after passing the mill wheel, was discharged into the Tring Drainage. The supply yields from 1 to 15 locks per day and when Tringford is full it can be diverted into Startopsend reservoir. Startopsend is also fed by the overflow from the adjoining Marsworth reservoir. Nowadays another source of supply for both Marsworth and Startopsend reservoirs is from the Tring sewage works. The works are situated between Marsworth reservoir and the Wendover branch and the supply produces about 4 locks per day.

The construction of the new reservoirs at Tringford and Startopsend saw the erection of a fourth pumping engine on the Wendover branch, this time at Tringford at a point selected by Thomas Telford. This new pumping station was destined to survive all the others and indeed to become the centralised station for the whole system of reservoirs on the Tring summit. From the station a heading was built to Tringford reservoir, whilst a branch of this heading served Startopsend. The work on the headings and on the two reservoirs was finally completed in the summer of 1817.[5] Meanwhile, earlier in the year, an order had been placed with Boulton & Watt for a steam engine. Pending delivery construction of the engine house was pushed ahead rapidly and by April 1818 this was nearly complete. Installation of the engine and pump then began and by the middle of August pumping had started. The engine cost £3,120.

Meanwhile in 1811, and again in 1827, the size of Wilstone reservoir was increased by raising its banks, bringing its total capacity to over 1,400 locks of water. In May 1835 work was started on a new reservoir,[6] which became known as Wilstone No 2, along the east side of the original Wilstone No 1 reservoir. The new extension was completed in January 1836. Wilstone No 2, which is the same size as No 1, is connected to No 1, and thus to the summit, by a paddle in the dividing bank. It has no natural supplies of its own and is fed from No 1 and partly by the overflow from Tringford and Startopsend reservoirs.

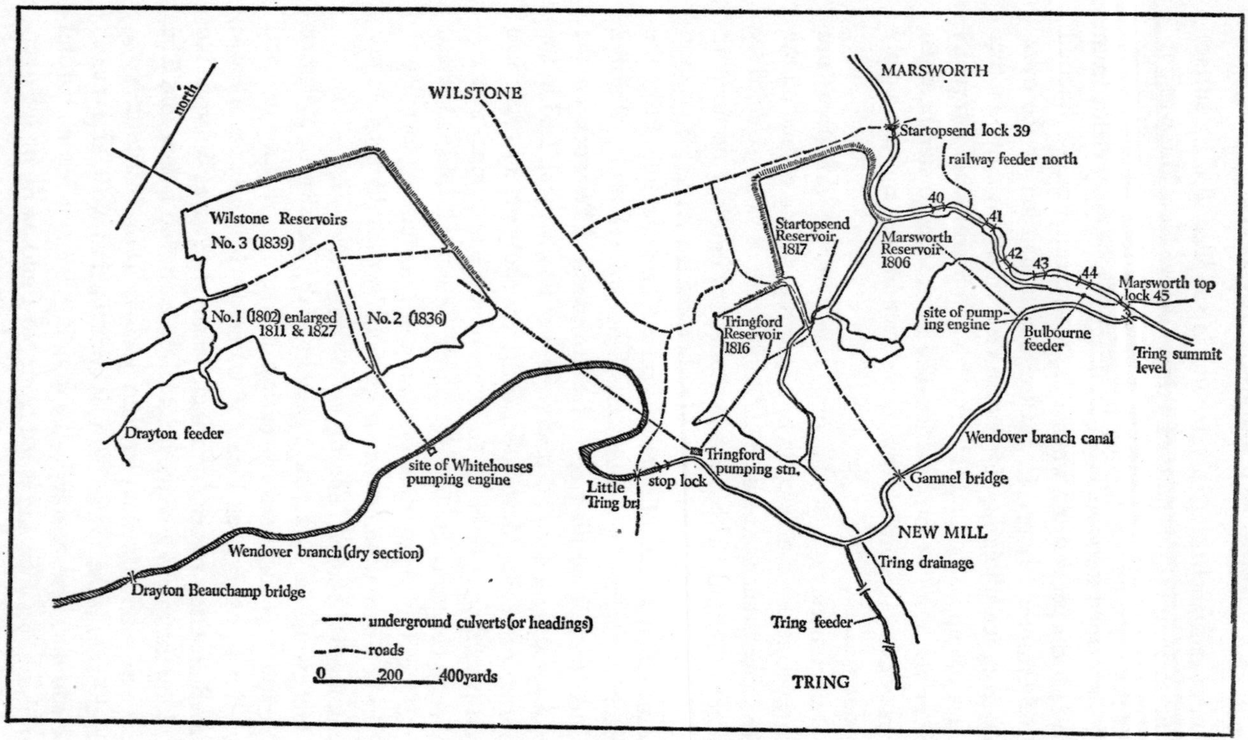

FIGURE 12. Tring reservoirs

Labels on map:

MARSWORTH

Startopsend lock 39
railway feeder north
40
41
42
43
44
Marsworth top lock 45
Tring summit level
Bulbourne feeder
Wendover branch canal
site of pumping engine
Marsworth Reservoir 1806
Gammel bridge
NEW MILL
Tring drainage
Startopsend Reservoir 1817
Tringford Reservoir 1816
Tringford pumping stn.
Little Tring br
Tring br
stop lock
Tring feeder
TRING

WILSTONE

Wilstone Reservoirs
No. 3 (1839)
No. 1 (1802) enlarged 1811 & 1827
No. 2 0836
site of Whitehouses pumping engine
Wendover branch (dry section)
Drayton feeder
Drayton Beauchamp bridge

north

underground culverts (or headings)
roads
0   200   400 yards

At the end of 1835, by which time the steam engine at White-houses was worn out and due for replacement, John Holland proposed that a new heading should be built from Wilstone to the Tringford pumping station.[7] This would enable the old engine at Whitehouses to be scrapped, whilst the new heading would not only tap additional water along its course but would also allow all the water to be pumped out as the existing heading to White-houses was not low enough for this to be done. Holland's sugges-tion was carried out, the driving of the half mile heading starting early in 1836. On account of the sheer magnitude of the work it was not until October 1837 that it was reported the task should be finished in five or six weeks time if a portion were left unlined with bricks. This course was adopted and pumping at Tringford from Wilstone started on 21 November 1837. The entire pumping operations were now centralised at one point.

Modifications had to be carried out to the Tringford engine to enable it to pump from the greater depth required, the lift from Wilstone varying from 60 to 75ft as compared with 35 to 50ft from Startopsend and 20 to 35ft from Tringford. The work, costing nearly £2,000, was carried out following a report in February 1836 by William Anderson, a consultant engineer advising the company. The modifications mainly consisted of building a new and deeper well shaft to link up with the heading from Wilstone and re-erecting the engine to draw from the new shaft. The original well shaft, which was connected to the heading to Tringford and Startopsend, was linked to the new shaft by a cross heading.

A further extension at Wilstone was now proposed and in October 1838 a tender from Hugh MacIntosh to build the exten-sion by contract was accepted, although it exceeded the estimate by nearly £1,000. Almost twice as large as the other two together, Wilstone No 3, which could hold 2,600 locks,[8] was completed in 1839. It lies to the north of the others and is connected to No 2 by paddles. At the same time a new overflow weir to serve the three reservoirs at Wilstone was built at the north-west corner of No 3 to enable water to be run into a nearby stream called

Gudgeon brook. There is a connection from this brook to the Aylesbury branch below lock 9, which allows the branch to be supplied from Wilstone if necessary. The old engine at White-houses was sold in April 1841, together with another old one, probably that formerly used at Weston Turville. The buildings of the pumping station at Whitehouses were converted into a dwelling house.

It was soon realised that with the concentration of all the pumping on one engine problems could arise during a break-down or normal repair works. So in December 1837, when Messrs Hunter & English, a well-known firm of engineers who had carried out some modifications to the Tringford engine in 1836, offered the company a second-hand pumping engine for £600, their proposal was accepted at once. The new engine, which became known as the 'York' engine, was installed in the original shaft or 'Old Pit' formerly occupied by the reconstructed 'Old' engine, which was now working in the 'New Pit'. The works were carried out in the summer of 1838 and at the same time preparatory works were carried out to deepen the Old pit and construct a separate low level heading to the shaft from the Wilstone heading, to enable the York engine to draw from Wilstone. It was found impossible to complete the job, however, without stopping the Old engine and when, in the following year, there was an enforced stoppage for repairs, the opportunity was taken to complete the works in the Old pit, the task being finished in June 1839.

In 1840 it was found that part of the foundations of the Old engine had sunk, thus causing another stoppage. William Cubitt was called in to inspect the damage and his investigations re-vealed that the brickwork of the foundations had literally been crushed by the repeated working of the engine. Remedial measures were taken, for the concussion caused at every stroke of the engine by a column of water weighing 14 tons was con-siderable. In November 1843 John Lake reported a serious acci-dent to the York engine, the trouble being caused when some nuts on the engine worked loose. Considerable damage resulted

Page 139　Southall: (*above*) Great Western Railway sleeper depot; (*below*) Maypole dock under construction, 1913

Page 140 Brentford: (above) Thames lock; (below) transhipping timber

and repairs were not finished until January 1841. This accident revealed a serious defect in the arrangement of the headings at Tringford, in that as the water from Startopsend and Tringford reservoirs had to come into the old well shaft under the York engine, no repairs to the York engine could be carried out whilst the Old engine was drawing from these reservoirs, and similarly once the repairs had started the Old engine could not pump from these reservoirs. Lake recommended a new 40yd long heading should be driven to allow water from the two reservoirs to enter the new well shaft under the Old engine, without having to pass through the Old pit, thus enabling either engine to work from either group of reservoirs independently. The new heading was built in four weeks and then the short interconnecting heading between the two well shafts was sealed off.

During all this time the problems of leakage from the Wendover feeder persisted and spasmodic repairs were carried out, but in 1841 it was found that 20 locks of water a day were being lost.[9] In 1844 Cubitt was called in to advise on the problem and it was decided to try and cure only the worst leaks, rather than repuddle the entire branch at a cost of about £12,000. Accordingly extra puddle was put in on both sides of the canal for 4½ miles at a cost of £2,654.[10] Before the work was carried out the company often had to close the Wendover feeder to trade by damming the branch and running the Wendover water down into the reservoirs. This caused considerable hardships to traders in Wendover, who had to divert their goods to Aylesbury, the company then having to pay them compensation.

Despite the money spent in 1844, ten years later the branch was leaking as badly as ever, a test in 1855 showing a loss of 25 locks each day.[11] One proposal was that the branch should be repuddled throughout at a cost at £12,500 and a little work was actually carried out. An alternative plan was then put forward, to line the canal bed with a layer of asphalt about 2½in thick. William Cubitt, who had been called in again, gave the proposal his backing and estimated the cost at £700 per mile as against the cost of repuddling at £2,700 per mile. The asphalting was com-

I

pleted in 1858, the worst stretch from Little Tring to Aston Clinton costing almost £6,500.[12] But the relief was only temporary; £555 had to be spent in 1860 on special repair works, whilst ten years later, when the leakage was worse than ever at almost 30 locks per day, further repairs to the asphalt and the puddle were carried out. In 1871 tests showed that 10 locks per day were being lost between Little Tring and Aston Clinton and 9 locks per day from Aston Clinton to Wendover. The tests also showed that the asphalt had cracked in places and had been damaged by boats rubbing against it. As a result the asphalt was removed from the worst sections and the puddle restored, the company charging £2,000 to reserve for this special work.[13] And so the struggle went on. The last major effort was made in 1895 and 1896 when £1,650 was spent on remedial measures.

Until 1838 the only significant water supply feeding directly into the summit, apart from the Wendover water, was from Bulbourne Head, where a spring fed into the canal about half a mile south of lock 45. During the building of the London & Birmingham Railway's cutting through the Chilterns near Tring the spring was diverted so that it no longer fed into the canal. The Grand Junction commenced a legal action against the London & Birmingham in March 1839, but in 1841 proceedings were suspended whilst the railway started building a culvert from just south of Tring station into the summit level about 200yd south of Marshcroft bridge, the high-level turnover bridge in the middle of the canal cutting. The culvert, known as the Railway Feeder South, drains the 1¼ miles of the southern end of the railway cutting and about 5 locks of water a day are obtained, although in summer the supply usually dries up completely.

The northern 1¾ miles of the railway cutting are drained by another culvert, the Railway Feeder North, which was constructed by the Grand Junction in 1838. Up to 30 locks per day have been obtained from this source. In May 1843 the dispute with the railway was finally patched up, the railway paying £5,200 in compensation and transferring to the Grand Junction the southern feeder together with the right to the water flowing both through this and the northern feeder. In fact the water in the northern railway feeder can be diverted into the Mottimore brook, which flows into the canal below lock 37, whilst part way along the culvert there is another connection with the canal just above lock 38. The culvert itself finally discharges into the pound between Marsworth locks 40 and 41, immediately opposite the weir into Marsworth reservoir. Indeed the Railway Feeder North forms the main supply to this reservoir.

In 1838, following an inspection and a report by William Anderson, construction of a series of pumping engines to return some of the lockage water, used on the north side of the summit, from the Ouse valley to the reservoirs was started. The engine houses and culverts were built by contractors Grissell & Peto for nearly £13,000 and by 1841 nine engines, which became known as the Northern Engines, had been installed to pass the water round the seventeen locks involved. The pumping stations were built at Fenny Stratford pumping round lock 22, at Stoke Hammond (lock 23), Soulbury (locks 24 to 26), Leighton Buzzard (lock 27), Church (locks 28 & 29), Horton (locks 30 & 31), Ivinghoe (locks 32 & 33), Seabrook (locks 34 to 36) and Marsworth (locks 37 & 38). The pumping stations were built of brick with slate roofs and were powered by steam engines.

From the pound above lock 38 the water could be run into Startopsend reservoir, whence it could be pumped to the summit by the Tringford engine. At one time the Marsworth engine pumped into the Railway Feeder North and hence into Marsworth reservoir, but the system was later modified for the water to enter the canal above lock 38, possibly because the railway feeder was too small to cope with the increased flow adequately. Not only did the Northern Engines return lockage water, but they also pumped from various streams which entered the canal to the north of the summit. The main supply is from Ledburn brook, which enters below Grove lock 28. Other streams are the Mottimore brook, the Pitstone brook which enters below Seabrook lock 35, a stream immediately below Soulbury three locks, another immediately above Stoke Hammond lock and a further one half a mile below this lock.[14]

As early as 1848 the Grand Junction had started on what was to prove a lengthy search for additional supplies to be drawn from wells. The first wells were sunk alongside Cowroast lock and a little further south at Dudswell. The Dudswell well was a failure but that at Cowroast became an important source of water, although its sinking brought the company into conflict with John Dickinson again. This dispute followed several dry summers, when many springs dried up completely as a result, it was claimed, of the company's pumping which had been nearly continuous. Dickinson brought an action contending the company had no right to well water and in January 1852 judgement was given against the company.[15] Some years later, during another dry spell, the springs dried up just the same. The millers, who were very short of water, appealed to the company which found that it was able to pump from its well, thus proving that the water came from another source. Thereafter the injunction was set aside by mutual consent.

Between 1859 and 1871 a well was sunk in Wendover and a portable steam engine obtained 9 locks per day. Permanent plant was considered, but as it was found that the well would deliver nearly 2 locks a day without any pumping, pipes were laid to feed the water by gravity to the branch. In 1874 and 1875 a second well was sunk but its yield was unsatisfactory until 1891, when a heading was built to the original well. The second well now yields from 1 to 4 locks a day.[16]

Between 1859 and 1862 a trial boring, which eventually reached 500ft, was made in Bulbourne works yard. This was unsuccessful and in 1896 another well was started at nearby Bulbourne Head on the site of the dried-up spring. By 1900 the well was 80ft deep with a boring of a further 146ft from the bottom, but the yield was poor and the work was abandoned. A proposal to deepen this well to 500ft in 1902 was not carried out. In 1855 and 1856 a well was sunk at Ivinghoe and a pump and beam engine installed to deliver the water to the canal. This well was successful and two more were sunk in 1864 connected to the original so that the pump could draw from them. Later, troubles were experienced at Ivinghoe with the wells filling with sand and although several attempts were made to clear them in the early 1900s they were only partially successful and the yield was disappointing.

The problems encountered on the Braunston summit, although often acute, have never been quite so complicated as on the Tring summit. Originally two reservoirs were built and several feeder streams were tapped. Braunston reservoir was extremely small, with a length of just over 300yd and a width of about 70yd. It had a top water area of slightly over 5 acres and lay immediately to the south of the canal midway between the top lock and the north-west end of the tunnel at Braunston. It had a very restricted catchment area, being fed by one small stream only and as a result was not very successful. Subsequently, and probably soon after the large Daventry reservoir was opened, Braunston reservoir was drained and the stream culverted under the headbank to enter the canal below water level. Later still the reservoir site was built across by the Weedon to Leamington railway, which was opened in 1895. The railway embankment across the reservoir was built only a few yards from and parallel to the old headbank, the stream being culverted under the railway as well.

The second reservoir on the Braunston summit is known as Drayton, or Daventry Old, reservoir; it lies alongside the west side of the Daventry to Kilsby road just south of the line of the tunnel. Drayton has a top water area of some 27 acres and a capacity of nearly 1,300 locks when full. It is fed by a stream from the west with a catchment area of over 500 acres, the outlet feeding into the summit alongside the south eastern portal of the tunnel. Another stream feeds into the northern tip of the reservoir. This stream has been culverted for most of its length from the north, and can only discharge into Drayton when the water level is several feet down. When the reservoir is full the stream can be diverted to feed directly into the summit.

With the rapid increase in traffic on the canal, even before the main line was properly completed, it was soon found that these two reservoirs were inadequate. It was finally decided to build a third and larger reservoir on part of the line of the proposed branch canal to Daventry. This, known as Daventry, or Daventry New, reservoir, lies to the east of the Daventry to Welton road half a mile south of the canal. The decision to go ahead was made in March 1803, following a report by Barker. He was told to open negotiations with the landowners for the purchase of the 75 acres needed, after which work was to start as soon as possible under Barnes' direction. Some of the land was on Daventry common, and its acquisition was delayed pending the passing of an Act for enclosing land around the town; work did not actually start until the middle of 1803.[17] In August it was decided to increase the size of the reservoir and Barnes and Barker were told to purchase the extra land needed. The reservoir was probably in use by the middle of 1804 but some work was still being carried out up to the end of the year. It cost about £20,000, of which over £9,000 was for the land required. Daventry originally had a capacity of 6,470 locks when full.[18] It has a water area of almost 100 acres and is fed by four streams running down the valley. The two main streams enter at the south-west end and they drain much of the town of Daventry, whilst a third enters immediately by the head-bank. The fourth stream, which enters on the eastern side, used to tap several small springs to the east of Daventry. Later some of these springs were used to provide supplies of drinking water and very little water now enters the reservoir from this source. The catchment area for the reservoir is over 2,100 acres and the outlet feeds into the summit level just over half a mile from the south-east end of the tunnel.

Both the Braunston and Drayton reservoirs had been started at the end of 1795, following a report by Jessop and Barnes in August, and both were finished by mid-1796 when the canal across the summit was opened. Shortly afterwards, in September 1796, Barnes was told to survey and set out a proposed feeder and reservoir from Watford to the main canal and to negotiate with the landowners concerned.[19] In November 1796 Barnes reported he had set out a 38 acre reservoir in the parishes of Welton and Ashby, but no further action was taken and instead work went ahead on the Watford feeder, which soon became an important source of supply to the summit.

At the south end of the Leicester line today there are three feeders—the Crick feeder which enters the Leicester line summit just south of Crick tunnel; the Watford feeder which enters from the west just below the Watford locks and the Old feeder, which enters, again from the west, just south of the Watling Street bridge. In addition the Welton feeder enters the Grand Junction summit from the north, just over 500yd east of Welton wharf. Originally and before the Grand Union Canal was built these four were all part of the Watford feeder, which entered the Grand Junction summit where the Welton feeder now comes in. The feeder took a somewhat roundabout course, virtually all on one level, following the contour and picking up several streams on the way, including the Crick water from the higher level at its northern end. There was a tunnel taking the feeder under some high ground at Weltonfield farm. But when the Grand Union was built its line crossed the feeder at two points, and it was decided to divide up the Watford feeder into a series of independent feeders. Parts of the line were abandoned, with most of the land reverting to its original owners, and minor alterations were carried out to make the various feeders flow into the new canal. For instance the Old feeder had its flow reversed for part of its length, whilst the Crick feeder was made to run directly into the Grand Union's summit. The Watford feeder of today has a catchment area of almost 2,800 acres and the Old feeder a catchment area of over 700 acres. In summer only a small supply is provided but in winter the feeders contribute a very significant source of water.

But even with the new Daventry reservoir in service shortages were still being felt on the summit and in April 1805 it was decided to erect a steam engine at the bottom of Braunston locks to pump water back. The engine was brought into service in the middle of June, having been transferred from Blisworth where it had been

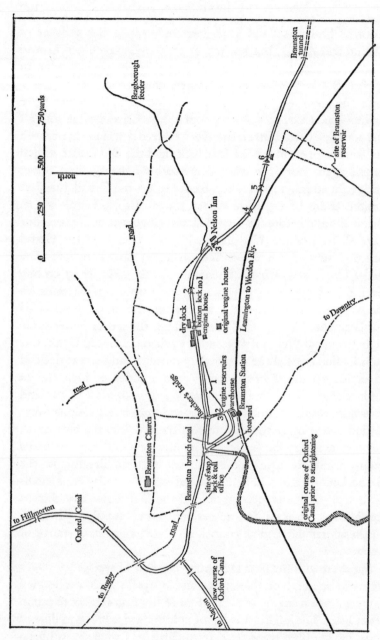

FIGURE 13. Braunston

used on the tunnel workings. The engine pumped from two small reservoirs, which were connected, provided alongside the canal at Braunston between the bottom lock and the junction with the Oxford canal. A channel led from the engine and eventually discharged into the summit just above the top lock. The reservoirs were supplied through a special paddle at the bottom lock, which discharged all the lockage water into them apart from the last 6in which went into the final stretch of the canal and hence into the Oxford canal. In addition to the steam engine another stream was tapped at this time to feed into the summit and side ponds were brought into use on the Buckby flight of locks to conserve water.[20] These works were all carried out under Barnes' supervision, for although he had left the company in June 1805 he was specially retained to see these works at Braunston, where he lived, through to their successful completion.

In September 1806 land was purchased for the building of a new wharf and warehouse at Braunston between the final stretch of the canal and the Daventry road. A short branch canal was planned at this time around the site of a third engine reservoir that was needed to provide more storage capacity. But it seems that only the reservoir was built at the time, with work on the branch being deferred. The first engine reservoir was extremely small, being less than half an acre; it was linked by an open channel to the second, just over one acre in size. When the third reservoir was built it was separated from the other two by a footpath and a culvert connection was provided. The third reservoir was nearly 2½ acres in size. There was never any connection with the waters of the main line,[21] and hence the Oxford canal, as both Oxford and Grand Junction companies guarded their own water jealously.

In 1810 the steam engine at Braunston was replaced by a new Boulton & Watt engine which lasted until 1896, when it was scrapped and a new Gwynnes steam pump was installed in a new engine house built alongside the canal below the bottom lock. The 1810 engine cost over £3,000 and was designed to pump 80 locks of water in 24 hours. At one time there was a proposal to extend the channel, into which the Braunston engine pumped, westwards along the contour to pick up several streams but this was never carried out.

There are several other small streams that supply the summit. One is the Welton Wharf feeder which enters the canal from Welton Place farm in the north just south of Welton bridge. Another small one enters from the west at the bottom of Buckby locks. This is the Norton feeder which, with another stream, drains land in Norton parish. The more northerly of the two supplies the canal, whilst the other passes under the canal in a culvert to link up with streams from Buckby and Murcott and eventually runs into the river Nene. Yet another is the Bragborough feeder, which enters the canal below the third lock at Braunston. At one time another very long channel was planned as an extension of the Watford feeder to enter the canal below Buckby bottom lock almost opposite the Norton feeder. This was to take a roundabout course, running parallel with a stream by way of Murcott, Long Buckby and Whilton mills. In April 1805 Barnes and Barker opened negotiations to try and purchase these mills in order to try and divert their water directly into the summit, but the talks failed and no action was taken on the proposed new feeder. In December 1806 the Warwick & Napton Canal company was considering a reservoir to hold 14,000 locks at Ashby St Ledgers, but the Oxford opposed the plan and the Grand Junction imposed so many conditions that it was dropped in February 1807.

The summit level at Braunston, nearly $3\frac{1}{2}$ miles long, is considerably deeper than the rest of the canal. In March 1805 Barnes was told to add four courses of brickwork to the two summit locks and a foot of boarding on the gates and to raise the banks and weirs where necessary to enable the summit level to be raised by 1ft when necessary. Braunston summit was originally built with a 2ft freeboard as against the more usual 1ft for the rest of the canal, and so raising the level presented few problems. This extra depth was to prove invaluable in many dry years that followed. In 1814 the Grand Union Canal was opened from its

junction with the Braunston summit to Foxton. As this had to
climb over a ridge, its water was passed into the Grand Junction.
But as most traffic moved on down from the Braunston summit
there was little advantage as far as water supplies were concerned.
By this time the Braunston supplies were on a much more secure
basis, with the reservoirs, feeders and pumping station providing
adequate capacity.

CHAPTER 7

The Railway Age

ALTHOUGH the Grand Junction and the canals in general represented a tremendous improvement in the existing inland transport facilities of the day, the waterways system was not ideal for the ever-increasing role it was called upon to play in the industrial revolution. One of the main drawbacks was that the system had developed piecemeal, with a multitude of companies each responsible for its own stretch of waterway, and there was virtually no overall co-ordinating policy. Most of the Midlands canals had been built to a standard size capable of taking a narrow boat, but throughout the country there were many anomalies that prevented the universal use of these boats. The Grand Junction had been built as a barge canal as had the Old Union, but the connecting Grand Union was narrow. Similarly the Northampton branch with its 7ft locks connected with the river Nene, which had barge locks, whilst the narrow locks on the canal routes to Birmingham and Coventry prevented the through working of barges. There were good reasons for building to these gauges at the time, but in the face of competition from newer forms of transport they proved considerable handicaps and the canal companies, lacking any common policy, proved incapable of ridding themselves of these problems.

Likewise there was not nearly enough concerted effort to try and simplify the toll system. Long-distance traffic was faced with a bewildering number of different companies to deal with and pay tolls to, which made the quoting of through rates extremely difficult. Not only this but relations between neighbouring companies were often poor, to say the least. Throughout their entire history the relationship between the Grand Junction and Oxford companies was usually hostile, the two looking on one another with mutual distrust. As a result, attempts at co-operation usually foundered, the Grand Junction voting against the Oxford's proposals and the Oxford against the Grand Junction's. Whilst the canals enjoyed a near monopoly the damage done by this disunity was not apparent, but in the face of a competitor it was a different matter.

As early as January 1823 the clerk to the Leeds & Liverpool Canal Co had written to the Grand Junction and other canal companies asking for their support in opposing the proposed application to Parliament to make a railway from Manchester to Liverpool. At the time railways were in their infancy, but the successful opening of the Stockton & Darlington line in September 1825 and the subsequent proving of the merits of the steam locomotive heralded an enormous challenge to the canals. The Grand Junction with its major trunk route to London was soon actively involved in the fray when, in 1824, the first proposal was made for a railway from London to Birmingham.[1] In fact this proposal was premature, but the idea did not die and another plan was put forward in the following year. This, too, failed, but a few years later the project was revived and this time it was more successful. Indeed by the summer of 1830 two proposals were being canvassed for a London to Birmingham railway.[2] The first, surveyed by Francis Giles, was for a line through Coventry, Rugby and Hemel Hempstead to terminate at Islington, whilst the other, which was surveyed by Sir John Rennie, was for a line through Banbury and Oxford. George and Robert Stephenson, called in to survey both, recommended the Coventry route, whereupon the two groups decided to join forces and promote an Act.[3] Robert Stephenson became the engineer and his route differed little from Giles' line; and as such it represented an enormous threat to the Grand Junction.

At the time an average of twenty-six fly boats a day in each direction on the canal carried the lighter and more perishable traffic,[4] and obviously it was feared that this would be the first to transfer to the railway, which promised to be so much faster, whilst there were also great numbers of ordinary canal boats carrying the bulk cargoes. So when the London & Birmingham Bill was presented to the Commons at the end of 1831 it met with a storm of vigorous opposition, not only from the Grand Junction, with whose line the railway was to run virtually parallel for many miles, but from a large number of landowners and from those who had their livelihood from the traffic on the roads. The busy Watling Street was directly threatened and road coach proprietors, waggoners and their supporting industries such as posting inns and stables all joined in the outcry. Much depended on the outcome of the London & Birmingham battle, for if the railway succeeded it would pave the way for further trunk lines throughout the country and in the fight in Parliament no holds were barred. At the beginning of June 1832 the Commons passed the Bill, but in July the Lords threw it out.[5]

The Grand Junction had been to the forefront of this opposition. At the start of 1832 there was an attempt to organise a united front against the railway scheme from all the canal companies affected, but even in the hour of danger there was disunity, the Birmingham Canal Co refusing to contribute to a general opposition fund. Thereafter the Grand Junction found its most powerful allies were the landowners and at the end of February the company allocated £2,000 towards the joint expenses of opposition. The Lords rejection provided only a temporary breathing space, for the Bill was re-presented in the next session and in the meantime the railway company was able to buy off most of the objecting landowners.[6] As a result, opposition in Parliament crumbled and the London & Birmingham Act was passed on 6 May 1833.

It is a great tribute to Jessop and Barnes that the London & Birmingham followed the canal line so closely. Like the canal the railway was to climb to a massive cutting through the Chilterns at Tring, and then followed a descent to Wolverton where the Great Ouse was crossed by a great embankment and a viaduct. Perhaps forewarned by the Grand Junction's epic struggle at

Blisworth, Stephenson decided to drive a cutting through the same ridge at nearby Roade. This proved a wise decision, for although he had a long and arduous struggle to complete the cutting, it was nothing to the difficulties a tunnel would have caused. In fact it was further north, at Kilsby, where Stephenson intended to drive a tunnel through the same hills that Braunston tunnel and Crick tunnel on the Grand Union pierced, that he had by far his worst problems. It seems that Stephenson had heard about the problems encountered at Crick (see Chapter 8) and moved his line further south to avoid the quicksands that had been found there, but he does not seem to have heard that the same quicksands were encountered when Braunston tunnel was being built, and the struggle that ensued at Kilsby soon made the Blisworth saga pale in contrast.

Despite these difficulties, the line from the London terminus at Euston to Boxmoor was opened in July 1837; from Boxmoor to Tring in October; from Tring to just north of Bletchley in April 1838 and finally through Roade cutting and Kilsby tunnel to Rugby in September 1838, whilst the line from Rugby to Birmingham was finished in April 1838. The railway crossed the canal six times: at Long Buckby, Blisworth, Wolverton, Cheddington, Winkwell and Nash Mill; and in several places the railway and canal ran particularly close: Long Buckby to Weedon; Bugbrooke to Blisworth, Soulbury to Leighton Buzzard and a long stretch from the Tring summit down to Hunton Bridge.

Naturally the Grand Junction did not go out of its way to be helpful to the railway which threatened its very existence. Under duress it did agree to an appeal by the railway for an extension from fifteen to twenty-eight days in the time allowed to build bridges over the canal. This was in February 1835, the decision being influenced by an incident at Wolverton in 1834. The railway wanted to build a temporary bridge over the canal which involved driving piles into the canal banks. The Grand Junction disputed the right to erect this bridge, nevertheless Stephenson assembled a strong work force and began building the bridge on the night of 23 December, the work continuing non-stop until the bridge was finished by midday on Christmas day. The Grand Junction was not prepared to ignore this provocative challenge and on 30 December Thomas Lake, the northern district engineer, headed a strong body of canal employees who proceeded to demolish the bridge completely.[7] The matter was only settled in the Court of Chancery in January, when the railway obtained an injunction to prevent the Grand Junction from destroying any of the railway works.

Once the London & Birmingham had been built, other lines quickly followed. A line from Cheddington to Aylesbury, and running virtually parallel to the Aylesbury branch canal, was opened in June 1839, whilst six years later a branch was opened from Blisworth to Northampton parallel with the Northampton branch canal. In November 1846 a line was opened from Bletchley to Bedford, crossing the canal at Fenny Stratford, and in May 1850 another from Bletchley was opened to Banbury via Buckingham. Further south a line from Leighton Buzzard to Dunstable was opened in May 1848, whilst still further south in the London area the canal was soon crossed by a veritable network of railways.

As had been expected, the railway's first gains were in the passenger and perishable goods traffic. Passenger movement had never been significant on the Grand Junction, but goods for which a speedy transit was essential formed a not unsubstantial trade on the canal. There was little the company could do about speed, where the railway had the obvious advantage, but in the heavy and slower moving bulk traffics where the railway's speed was little advantage the two rivals were soon involved in a cut-throat rates battle. The Grand Junction's tonnage revenue had reached its peak in 1836; from 1 January 1837 substantial reductions were made, causing the revenue to drop by nearly a quarter. General goods were reduced by 25 per cent from 16s 10¾d per ton to 12s 7½d (84½p–63p) and coal was reduced to ¾d per ton per mile with a maximum of 4s 4½d (22p) per ton or a maximum of 2s 1¼d (10½p) if brought all the way to London. At the same time certain regulations were amended so that the canal was now open twenty-four hours a day and mixed cargoes were permitted. From

31 March 1839 there was another major reduction, the maximum rate now being 1d per ton per mile. This sharp drop in revenue continued until 1846, but thereafter the decline slowed down considerably for the next twenty years. The figures from 1837 to 1874 averaged over three year periods are as follows:

Years	Toll Receipts £	Years	Toll Receipts £
1837–9	148,879	1858–60	67,777
1840–2	118,635	1861–3	71,861
1843–5	115,269	1864–6	75,787
1846–8	82,592	1867–9	66,983
1849–51	81,633	1870–2	60,061
1852–4	79,930	1873–4*	66,842
1855–7	72,029		* two years only

In fact the drop in revenue would have been even more marked if it had not been for the upsurge in tonnage carried at this time. This arose from the ever-growing demand for transport from the increasingly industrialised country, and particularly from the Black Country centred on Birmingham, to London. The railways soon captured the lion's share of this new traffic, but the Grand Junction managed to retain its position as an important artery of trade. An example of the growth of traffic from industry was in iron from Staffordshire and Shropshire carried on the canal to London.[8]

	1815	1820	1825	1830	1835	1840
Manufacturing Iron	14,900	17,722	15,258	17,338	25,427	43,613
Pig iron	2,832	5,208	3,471	1,289	420	1,254
Cast Iron Pipes	2,475	445	905	—	—	—
Castings	3,240	8,237	9,901	8,205	13,542	10,736
Wrought Iron Bedsteads	—	—	581	58	4	91
Total	23,447	31,612	30,116	26,890	39,393	55,694

Considering the drastic nature of the toll cuts it is surprising how the revenues managed to hold up after the first very sharp fall. A major drop of £17,000 in 1845 was caused by the halving of the main through toll between London and Braunston to ½d per ton per mile, whilst a small rise in the 1849 revenues was

K

probably due to the rate being raised to $\frac{3}{4}$d per ton per mile for most articles in February of that year.[9] By this increase it was hoped to attract £11,500 in revenue if the traffic remained the same, whilst a new tariff introduced in September 1848 was estimated to produce £4,100 in a full year. On the whole, however, reductions were the order of the day. In October 1844, for instance, the toll between London and Northampton was reduced to 4s 2½d (21p) per ton, whilst in March 1846 this figure was halved. To try and stimulate coal traffic the toll was reduced to $\frac{1}{2}$d per ton per mile in August 1847, but with a maximum of 2s 1¼d (10½p) per ton, and in September 1850 this maximum was further reduced to 1s 6d (7½p) for coals to London.[10] This compared with 4s 9½d (24p) which was being charged in 1836, which in itself was exactly half the toll authorised by Parliament.

The traffic in coal from Braunston to the London area had been 72,256 tons in 1844 but this had fallen to 60,311 in the following year.[11] At the time the railways' carryings were minute, a mere 8,377 tons in 1845, probably due to the initial reluctance of the London & Birmingham to carry it. This was soon overcome, whereupon the railway's share increased by leaps and bounds; to 55,096 tons in 1850 against the canal's 29,479 tons, to 1,137,835 tons in 1855 (23,251 tons) and 1,477,547 tons in 1860 (19,593 tons), until by 1867 the tonnage brought by rail, 3,295,652 tons mainly by the London & North Western Railway (formerly the London & Birmingham) and the Great Northern Railway, exceeded the sea coal tonnage, which had been fairly static between two to three million tons, for the first time.[12] By now the canal's share had fallen below 10,000 tons.

Accurate figures for coal were kept because of the London Coal Duties Acts, to which the railways were subject as was the Grand Junction. The boundary for these duties was originally computed as being 25 miles from the General Post Office in London, but in 1845 the distance was altered to 20 miles. It seems, however, that the Grand Junction collector remained at Grove. In 1861 the dues area was amended again to include only places in the Metropolitan police district. On the canal this made the boundary a short way below Stockers lock and a stone obelisk was erected beside the towpath to mark the position. The collector now moved from Grove to a new house that had been built for him beside the lock,[13] but the money raised by the dues on canal-borne coal was falling rapidly, in line with the tonnage. In August 1863 the canal dues yielded about £36, whereas railborne coal produced £7,132 and seaborne £14,552. In 1869, therefore, it was decided to discontinue the appointment of a collector at Stockers, the company undertaking to collect the dues from 1870 for an annual fee of £35.[14] The coal dues finally came to an end in 1890.

One effect of the railway age had been the stimulation of interest in an improved canal route from London to Liverpool. Part of the plan, the Birmingham & Liverpool Junction Canal, was opened in 1835. Southwards from Birmingham a project was first announced in November 1827 for the London & Birmingham Junction Canal, to run from the Stratford-upon-Avon Canal about 10 miles south of Birmingham to the Grand Junction at Braunston,[15] with Telford as engineer. The line was to pass under the Oxford Canal, and there was to be a branch to the Coventry Canal. The great advantage of this line was that it avoided heavy lockage into and out of the Avon valley at Warwick that was such a handicap to the canal route. Only twenty locks were needed, against nearly eighty by the Warwick canals, whilst the Coventry branch would have reduced the through route to the north by 10 miles by cutting out the circuitous northern section of the Oxford. Not unnaturally the Oxford company strongly opposed the plan and was joined by the two Warwick canals and the Trent & Mersey, who all stood to lose traffic. This plan did stir the Oxford into straightening and improving its northern section and in view of this the line for the London & Birmingham Junction was amended in 1828 to run to the Oxford at Ansty. Two years later, with the termination altered to Brinklow, a Bill was put forward in February 1830, but was thrown out in May. The idea did not die, although Telford ceased to take any interest, his place being taken by William Cubitt, who had been consulted about the straightening of the Oxford, and in 1832 he produced plans for a Central Union Canal to run from the Worcester & Birmingham in Birmingham to Bordesley, on the Warwick & Birmingham, and then from Solihull to Ansty.[16]

This plan, too, got nowhere but at the end of 1833 a group of promoters, it seems with the backing of Lord Dudley and other Staffordshire coal and ironmasters who opposed the restrictive toll agreements then in force between the Coventry and Warwick canals, planned the London & Birmingham Canal. The line, which was surveyed by James Green, was to run from the Stratford-upon-Avon Canal to pass through Banbury, Buckingham, cross the Grand Junction near Tring, and run to St Albans and Highgate, where a branch was to link up with the Regent's Canal. In all, it was to be 113 miles long with 48 locks, and a further 22 locks on the Regent's Canal branch. From the Stratford Canal there were to be 19 locks and then a level pound of over 70 miles to St Albans. But nearly 10 miles of tunnelling would be needed as well as an enormous aqueduct over the Avon valley, whilst the cost was estimated at about £3,000,000.[17] A prospectus issued in March 1836 envisaged an elaborate set up. Where tunnelling was necessary twin tunnels each with a towing path were to be made, the sides of the canal were to be walled and a double towing path was to be provided throughout. It was claimed that goods would be delivered in London in thirty-two hours instead of seventy by the existing route.[18]

Naturally, the Grand Junction opposed the whole idea and in 1836 compromise proposals were put forward involving junctions at either Stoke Bruerne, Weedon or Braunston, thence using the Grand Junction line to London. These were all rejected and in the following year a plan to join the Buckingham branch was also turned down.[19] Not only were rival canal companies disenchanted with the scheme, but the promoters found it impossible to raise the capital needed, which was scarcely surprising as the current vogue was then investment in railways. There was a final meeting in Cubitt's London office in March 1838 but thereafter the plan for a new canal line seems to have died a natural death. But, just as the earlier London & Birmingham Junction scheme had spurred the Oxford to improve the northern part of its line, so this latest project stimulated the Grand Junction into making improvements to its own line. At the beginning of 1835 a proposal was put forward for doubling the Stoke Bruerne flight of locks to speed up the traffic and also save water in the long Blisworth pound, which had to supply the Northampton branch as well. A detailed plan had been drawn up by William Thompson and John Holland and the work was given the go-ahead in March. Duplicate wide locks were provided alongside each of the seven existing locks on the west side, the road bridges at the tail of the top lock in Stoke Bruerne village and below lock 18 being given a double waterway arch.

Three years later, in January 1838, it was decided to purchase land at Marsworth and build duplicate narrow locks parallel to locks 37 to 45 on the northern descent from the Tring summit. In June William Cubitt was asked to tender for building them, but his figure was evidently too high, for Messrs Grissell & Peto were asked to tender at the end of June, and got the job. Once the Marsworth locks had been duplicated the decision was taken to extend the duplication all the way down to Stoke Hammond; the whole series was virtually completed by the middle of 1839. Six bridges, all either immediately above or below a lock, had to be provided with a double waterway arch and these remain to this day. In all, 23 locks northwards from the summit were duplicated, but Fenny Stratford lock was not, probably because of its very small rise. The main reason for this duplication was to speed up the single narrow boat traffic, which at the time made up a high proportion of the boats using the canal. In the company's original Act boats of less than 60ft in length, 12ft in width and carrying less than 30 tons could be prevented from passing along the canal unless there was a surplus of water. When there was a water shortage single narrow boats often had to wait until they could find a partner to pass through the wide locks, unless they were prepared to pay extra charges. The number of single narrow boats was quite substantial and in December 1836 a new and reduced tariff had been introduced, which relaxed the restrictions. In the years that followed, whenever there was a water shortage, as in December 1837, the restrictions were reimposed but they did not apply when the narrow locks were used. In October 1837 the company also considered providing narrow locks southwards from the Tring summit to Hunton Bridge, but disagreements with the millers at Kings Langley prevented the work being carried out.

Neither the duplicate narrow locks nor the duplicate wide ones at Stoke had a long life. The water supply situation, particularly at Tring, was soon much improved with the third Wilstone reservoir and the chain of pumps from Fenny Stratford in service, and there was also a trend away from singles to pairs of boats. After a while the locks north of Tring were filled in and with modern bank protection work most traces of them have completely disappeared. Similarly at Stoke five of the duplicates were filled in, but at the top and bottom of the flight they were used to make side ponds, and many years later, in the 1960s, the duplicate top lock was used to house a boat weighing machine as part of the museum established there. Side ponds were provided for the other five locks, the working drawings being prepared by Jesse Cherry, the northern district engineer, in 1852. One other result of the proposed London & Birmingham Canal was the agreement by the Grand Junction to reduce its tolls from 1837.

Mounting railway competition soon spotlighted the lack of unity amongst the various canal companies and the poor relations between the Grand Junction and the Oxford companies. At the end of the 1830s the Grand Junction was putting out feelers to other companies to see if they would co-operate in toll reductions to stimulate through traffic. At first there was little success, the others blaming the Grand Junction's water shortages, which were often acute, for the difficulties the trade was then facing. In May 1841, when the Grand Junction's water position was better, there was a meeting of the through route companies, with the exception of the Oxford who refused to attend, at which it was hoped to arrange a standard through toll of $\frac{1}{4}$d per ton per mile. At the time the tolls between Manchester and London were:

Canal	miles	s	d	
Bridgewater Canal	25	1	0	($\frac{1}{2}$d p.t.p.m.)
Trent & Mersey Canal	67	2	9$\frac{1}{2}$	($\frac{1}{2}$d p.t.p.m.)
Coventry (Fradley section)	5$\frac{1}{2}$		2$\frac{3}{4}$	($\frac{1}{2}$d p.t.p.m.)
Birmingham (Fazeley section)	5$\frac{1}{2}$		5$\frac{1}{2}$	(1d p.t.p.m.)
Coventry Canal	21$\frac{1}{4}$		11	($\frac{1}{2}$d p.t.p.m.)
Oxford Canal	23$\frac{5}{8}$	2	11	(1$\frac{1}{2}$d p.t.p.m.)*
Grand Junction Canal	101	4	2$\frac{1}{2}$	($\frac{1}{2}$d p.t.p.m.)
	248$\frac{7}{8}$	12	6$\frac{1}{4}$	

* 1d per ton per mile if calculated on the Oxford's original mileage
   before the major straightening operations

Without co-operation from the Oxford and to a lesser extent from the Birmingham no progress was made. A copy of the minutes of the meeting was sent to the Oxford, but it produced no effect. The Grand Junction renewed the attack at a joint meeting of canal companies to which the Oxford was at last persuaded to send delegates, claiming that the Oxford was still charging 1$\frac{3}{4}$d per ton mile on the coal trade to London whereas the Grand Junction was only charging $\frac{1}{4}$d per ton mile. The Oxford retorted that the Grand Junction's rate was a special one that applied to the London trade only and that its own rate was based on its original mileage and no other charge had ever been made for the convenience of using its shortened line; but the Oxford's particular bone of contention was that it felt the Grand Junction favoured the Leicester canals through its special relationship with the Grand Union company. Certainly the two Leicester companies were usually willing to co-operate with the Grand Junction, and from 1 May 1845 a general reduction to $\frac{1}{2}$d per ton per mile was agreed for all goods to and from the Leicester line, which placed similar goods entering at Braunston at a disadvantage, since until the Oxford agreed to reduce, the Grand Junction refused to extend the new rates to it.

The Grand Junction kept trying and in May 1846 an approach

was made to the Warwick canals with a view to a merger. The Warwick companies were willing to negotiate and at the same time the idea of bypassing the Oxford with a new canal was considered. Thomas Lake estimated that £72,914 would be needed for a canal just over 6 miles long from the third lock at Braunston to join the Warwick & Napton near Napton. This must have disturbed the Oxford, as did a suggestion for a similar link up with the Leicester canals and a new flat rate of ¼d per ton per mile all the way to London, but with all traffic leaving the Oxford being at the same rate as the Oxford was charging. Although this would have harmed the Grand Junction it would have crippled the Oxford by putting a stop to the thriving coal trade from the Warwickshire collieries. After some more procrastinating the Oxford relented and eventually a comprehensive toll agreement was arrived at after a series of arduous negotiations between Sir Francis Head, then the Grand Junction's chairman, and Mr Durrell of the Oxford.

Apart from its efforts at organising general toll reductions with other companies, the Grand Junction was also to the fore when in 1853 it arranged a meeting of canal concerns to consider what should be done about railway and canal mergers. At the time the merging of several railway companies, who also controlled some canals, was in prospect and this could have had a very retrograde effect on the canal system as a whole. As usual the Oxford was unco-operative, mainly it seems because the Grand Junction was involved, and appeared to prefer railway domination rather than anything likely to benefit the Grand Junction in any way. There was another get-together in the following year, when a maximum toll of ½d per ton mile was fixed on all goods passing into or out of the Grand Junction at either Braunston or Long Buckby. By this time, of course, most of the tolls were already well under this maximum. Other companies involved in this agreement were the Oxford, Coventry, Grand Union, Old Union, Leicester Navigation, Warwick & Napton and Warwick & Birmingham.

Meanwhile the trend of tolls continued downward and an attempt to increase that on the Birmingham trade to 12s 7½d (63p) per ton in May 1849 resulted in one of the larger carrying firms, Shiptons, leaving the canal.[20] The company relented at the end of the year and enticed Shiptons back by reducing the toll to 6s 3¾d (31½p), but it was a short-lived return for in the middle of 1853 Shiptons carried their last freight to and from London and finally left the canal; their tolls had produced £3,014 in 1852.[21]

In November 1851 the Warwick & Napton compensation toll, which dated back to the very first days of the concern, was abolished. Originally the Warwick & Napton, or the Warwick & Braunston as it was first called, was to have joined the Grand Junction at Braunston, thus completing the by-passing of the entire Oxford line on the route from Birmingham to London. The Oxford had been compensated by the £10,000 guarantee of revenue given it in the original Grand Junction Act. But in 1795 the Warwick & Braunston decided to apply to Parliament for permission to alter its eastern end to join the Oxford at Napton, to save 4 miles of canal and £62,000 in expenses. The Grand Junction naturally felt that in these changed circumstances its guarantee to the Oxford should be modified, although it did suggest that if the Warwick & Braunston would construct its canal as a wide waterway it could afford to forget the question of compensation, as the advantages that would accrue would more than make good the difference.[22] The Warwick & Braunston would not agree to this and included in its second Act, passed in May 1796, were the same compensation tolls to the Oxford as in the Grand Junction Act—2s 9d (14p) on coal and 4s 4d (21½p) on other goods passing between the Warwick & Napton and the Grand Junction to be used to help satisfy the Grand Junction's £10,000 liability. Also included in the Act was a further compensation toll of 6d (2½p) per ton on all goods passing into and out of the Warwick & Napton at Napton, which the Grand Junction was authorised to collect; the company being given power to erect a toll house on the Warwick & Napton within 100yd of the junction with the Oxford. The Grand Junction's £10,000 obligation to the Oxford was repealed in 1829 in an Act authorising the shortening of the Oxford line northwards from Wolfhampcote near Braunston and finally came to an end from 31 March 1832.

Naturally railways had a marked effect on the price of the Grand Junction shares. In the company's earliest days they had a high speculative value and often attracted a large premium. In September 1792 ten shares of £100 each, with only £1 paid up, were sold for 430 guineas,[23] but the company's financial problems in its first ten years tended to level the price out and by 1800 the shares were being exchanged at par. There was a small rise over the next few years until by 1807 a modest premium of £10 per share was being attracted. Thereafter the demand and hence the price moved steadily upwards in pace with the increasing dividend; £240 in 1810, £320 in 1811, £280 in 1812. There was a temporary drop in 1816, when the dividend was cut, with the price nearly back to par, but by 1824 a record price of almost £350 was being obtained. The price declined to £312 in 1827 and £295 in 1829, with a sharp fall to £236 in 1830 as investors turned to railway schemes. Ten years later the price was half this, but thereafter it rallied and remained around par for many years. Similarly the dividend maintained its peak of 13 per cent for seven years until 1832 when it declined to 12 per cent. It retained this level until 1838 when it dropped to 10 per cent and then it tumbled to touch 5 per cent in 1847 and 2 per cent in 1855. But from the 1860s it stabilised itself at 4 per cent, at which level it remained unchanged for many years.

The drop in the share price and dividend reflected heavy rate cutting by both canals and railways; by the 1850s rates had reached a very low level. However, it seems that both the London & North Western and Great Western railways, the two companies principally concerned with the Grand Junction, were feeling the pinch, for an agreement in 1857 put an end to the rate cutting and stabilised tolls. It must have been greeted on all sides with relief. For the Grand Junction this meant that most goods between London and Braunston were charged a maximum of $\frac{1}{4}$d per ton mile, or 2s 1$\frac{1}{4}$d (10$\frac{1}{2}$p) for the full journey. Thereafter most alterations were for specific items; for instance the toll on iron was reduced to a net 2s (10p) per ton from 1 January 1866, costing about £4,000 in lost revenue for a full year, whilst in January 1868 ashes, breeze and bricks went down 2d per ton, with an estimated loss of £2,500 to the company. But despite these reductions the revenue remained remarkably buoyant, indicating that more tonnage was still being attracted, although it contributed proportionately less in tolls. As a result of the railway agreement one method the company used to try and stimulate trade, the granting of drawbacks, was used far less frequently. A drawback was, in effect, a discount on tolls granted by the company to traders to encourage the carriage of specific goods. It was often linked to a minimum tonnage.

Meanwhile the spread of the railway network continued. In July 1840 the Midland Counties Railway between Leicester and the London & Birmingham's line at Rugby was finished; this provided a direct railway link between the Derbyshire and Nottinghamshire coalfield and London. Another route was forged in April 1857 when the Midland railway from Leicester through Bedford to Hitchin, where it joined the Great Northern line to London, was opened. The carriage of coal off the Midland by both Rugby and Hitchin was soon very heavy, so much so that the Midland opened its own direct line from Bedford to London in 1868. In this work the Grand Junction made its presence felt by insisting on a long viaduct over the Brent valley at Hendon, where the Brent reservoir lay. To cater for the coal traffic a basin was opened at St Pancras on the Regent's Canal, where coal could be transhipped from rail wagons to canal boats. From the Midland at Harpenden a line to Hemel Hempstead was opened in 1877, crossing the canal just below Boxmoor bottom lock. This must have taken traffic, particularly in coal, from the Grand Junction. Further south a stretch of the Great Western Railway had been opened in June 1838 virtually parallel to the canal between Paddington and Yiewsley. From this a branch from Yiewsley to Uxbridge was opened in September 1856. The Brentford Railway from Southall to Brentford followed in July 1859 together with a dock by the river Thames to transfer goods

between barges and the railway. At the time of the opening of the
Brentford line the Grand Junction reckoned that it would lose
about £4,200 at Brentford and Bulls Bridge toll stations. The
Brentford line is noteworthy in that it passes under the canal at
the same spot as the canal passes under Windmill Lane in Norwood, thus making a three-level intersection. The Great Western
built a dock on the canal at Hayes alongside the present Hayes &
Harlington station, and from about 1856 regular transhipment
from the railway to barges started, for delivery to destinations
along the Paddington branch and the Regent's Canal. The Great
Western also established a sleeper depot alongside the Paddington branch at Southall, which was supplied with timber from
London docks that was carried up the Grand Junction by
barge.

Two small sections of the Grand Junction were actually taken
over by a railway and built upon. On the Paddington branch at
Wormwood Scrubbs, under an agreement with the Birmingham,
Bristol & Thames Junction Railway, later the West London
Railway, in May 1839 a portion of the canal bed was used for the
railway, whilst the railway company purchased other land on
which to divert the canal. The work was carried out, but the railway was somewhat dilatory in completing the purchase of the
land for the canal and still had not paid in January 1842 when the
original owners served an ejectment notice on the unfortunate
Grand Junction. This notice was withdrawn after a few weeks,
the aggrieved owners seeking redress from the guilty railway
company. At first the West London line passed underneath the
canal but, in 1858, plans were agreed for the line to be diverted
northwards and to cross over it instead.

The second section was at Northampton, where in 1876 the
London & North Western Railway obtained powers to construct
a connecting line to enable trains from the main Northampton
Castle station to link up with the Blisworth to Peterborough line
in an easterly direction. This involved filling in the Northampton
branch from just over one furlong below lock 16 to the head of
lock 17. The canal did not suffer, however, as a diversion was

constructed and brought into service during June 1879, the railway paying £1,500 as compensation.

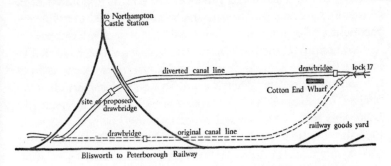

FIGURE 14. The deviation by the LNWR, at Northampton

Another way in which the Grand Junction tried to compete with the railways was in carrying. In the early days most canal companies were reluctant to carry on their own waterways, since by so doing it was possible for them to give preferential rates that would be equivalent to varying the tolls, which was then illegal. The Grand Junction was no exception, and although it owned trading boats throughout its existence these were usually for hiring out to other traders. In 1845 the legal position was cleared up by the Canal Carriers Act, and at the same time varying tolls was made legal.

Initially the Grand Junction was disinclined to change its policy, but a major upheaval at the June 1847 half-yearly shareholders meeting resulted in the removal of Sir Francis Bond Head as chairman, his replacement by Thomas Grahame, and the appointment of an almost new select committee. This change of management coincided with similar changes on the Grand Union Canal. The two were probably connected, since the Grand Junction was considering purchasing the Grand Union at the time, but it seems the Grand Junction's upset was also affected by an internal row as to whether the company should set up as carriers. Thomas Grahame was a strong supporter and his appointment was timely as Pickfords, who were still the most important carrying concern on the canal, decided to give up their canal carrying business altogether at the end of 1847 and go over to the railways. The Grand Junction had already appointed B. P. Gregson as manager of the canal and the proposed carrying department in August and the potential loss of such a large part of its trade removed the last objections. The shareholders agreed to form a Carrying Establishment, special rates were secured from the companies on the Warwick and Leicester lines and Gregson opened negotiations to take over not only most of Pickfords' boats and traffics but several other carrying businesses as well. Probably the first acquired was that of Messrs Wheatcroft at the end of November 1847. These boats were joined soon afterwards by the Pickfords' fleet, the company taking over the important Manchester trade from the beginning of 1848. The extent of Pickfords' business can be judged from figures for the nine months to March 1848:

Goods carried from Manchester (75 tons per day)	23,475 tons
Goods carried from London (35 tons per day)	10,955 tons
Intermediate traffic	32,355 tons
Goods carried in other carriers' boats	17,215 tons
	84,000 tons

In December 1847 the new Carrying Establishment's fleet numbered 30 boats, but by March 1848 this had risen to over 200. Further acquisitions followed, three businesses being taken over in October 1848: Messrs Soresby of Derby who operated 9 narrow boats, 35 boat horses and 5 dray horses; Worster & Co of Long Buckby who had 7 boats, 35 horses, and 8 delivery vans at Northampton, 9 at the City Road Basin on the Regent's Canal and 2 each at Market Harborough and Long Buckby; and John Whitehouse & Sons of Dudley who operated 16 boats, 25 horses and 11 waggons. Other carriers such as Crowley & Co, Corbett & Sons, and in January 1849 Job Bissell with 23 boats, were then acquired to be followed in August 1849 by the business of William Ebbern, who traded between London and the Potteries. In several cases the former owners agreed to carry on as agents for the company, which soon built up a chain of depots often some way from the Grand Junction, such as at Derby, Burton, Lichfield, Tipton, and Warwick. In September 1848 a wharf in Leicester was leased from the Old Union Canal Company and in December a wharf and premises at Lower Fazeley Street in Birmingham was rented from the Warwick & Birmingham. An agent was appointed in the Potteries in March 1849 and in the following month land was bought for a wharf at Wolverhampton. At the London end the business was based initially on Paddington Basin, but several of the carriers taken over, such as Worster & Co and Crowley & Co, operated from City Road Basin, so in April 1849 the company moved its carrying operations from Paddington to the City Road.

To finance all this activity £114,550 of a new 6 per cent preference stock was issued to the existing shareholders in the proportion of £10 of new stock for every £100 ordinary share held. The first call of 25 per cent was made on 1 September 1848, the second on 1 January 1849 and the other two soon afterwards. Thomas Morris was appointed traffic manager from 1 February 1850 at £500 pa, increased to £800 from June 1852.

With this tremendous expansion a large proportion of the Grand Junction's total trade was soon being handled by the Carrying Establishment. In 1851 £29,100 was contributed to a total revenue of £79,600 and this rose to a peak of £31,700 in 1853. But no profits were being earned from carrying and the company became disenchanted with Gregson, who left in the autumn of 1850. The reason was probably the £12,800 loss turned in by the carrying side for the half year to June 1850, against a profit of £25,800 on the ordinary canal account. A proposal to reduce the dividend to 1 per cent was only defeated on the questionable grounds that the carrying side was now on a firmer footing. Six months later the deficit was down to £1,500, but interest on the preference stock and on debts to the main company totalled a further £3,100. At this time the Carrying Establishment's debt to the company was almost £31,000 and a start was made on writing this off, the carrying side being relieved of the interest payments, and surplus funds from the canal account after payment of dividend being applied to extinguish the debt. In June 1852 the remaining debt of £17,000 was written off completely.

Although thought had been given to reducing the scale of the carrying business, operations remained very substantial. In June 1853 the company had 510 boat horses and 136 cart horses and in the half year to 25 June handled 85,750 tons with receipts of £80,500. This compared with 68,260 tons and receipts of £68,300 in 1852. To cope with this increase several batches of new boats were built, new stables were provided at Bulls Bridge, Rickmansworth, Dudswell and Norton and experiments made with a new steam tug. But plenty of difficulties remained. In April 1853 the beer trade from Bass's brewery at Burton to London was lost to the railways; there were several strikes amongst the boatmen at City Road and in June 1854 the fly-boat captains demanded an 8s (40p) per voyage rise, which would have cost £4,000 a year. Thomas Morris resigned at the end of September 1854 and was not replaced at first, George Anderson, who had taken over as chairman of the company in June 1854, assuming responsibility for the carrying side.

From 1855, following continuing concern about losses, the carrying operations were scaled down considerably. The depot at Limehouse opened in 1851, which had proved a costly luxury, was reduced, much of the traffic being diverted to Brentford. The work of the company's two boatyards at City Road and Birmingham was suspended early in 1855 when craft repairs and the building of new boats was contracted out to William Camwell at Braunston; more fundamental still, in March negotiations were opened to transfer part of the Birmingham trade to Price & Sons and Messrs Fellows. Agreement was reached in April for 13,000 tons of heavy castings to be diverted to them. Early in 1856 Mellor, Colsell & Co took over the cheese and pottery trade to London and purchased eighteen boats for this purpose and in 1865 this same firm took over the Manchester trade as well. These

Page 173 (above) The experimental inclined plane built at Bulbourne depot, 1896; (below) the approach to the top of Foxton incline

Page 174 (*above*) The bottom of Foxton inclined plane; (*below*) a steam dredger near Yelvertoft, 1896

transfers were reflected in the sums paid by the Carrying Establishment to the Grand Junction which dropped to £23,400 in 1855, below £20,000 in 1856 and below £13,000 in 1866.

Following a visit by the chairman to inspect steam tugs on the Leeds & Liverpool and Forth & Clyde Canals in 1859, the company fitted one of its own boats with a steam engine and screw propeller for £300. In December 1860 *Pioneer* had produced such satisfactory results that two more tugs were ordered together with nine carrying boats all equipped with steam engines. The tugs were for service between Paddington and Cowley on the Long Level, but the other boats entered the ordinary carrying fleet, and to pay for them £4,000 was borrowed from Praed & Co, the company's bankers. The boats were a considerable success, although almost £1,000 had to be paid out in July 1863 to Dickinson's for damage caused at Home Park Mill when a spark from the steamer *Foam* set fire to piles of paper shavings. There were also complaints about damage caused to canal banks, as in July 1864 when the Leicester Navigation agreed to accept £105 to settle its damages claim. A more serious complaint was made in 1861 by the Regent's Canal Company about the carriage of gunpowder in these boats. Nothing was done at the time, but there were grave repercussions later.

On the other hand, the Carrying Establishment was still making a loss and in 1864 a proposed merger with the Warwick canals had to be called off because they were unwilling for the enlarged concern to continue carrying. For its part the Grand Junction was reluctant to give up carrying because of the large amount of trade that would be lost, for the carrying side had been successful in maintaining traffic. In 1835 total tonnage was 824,674, of which through traffic accounted for 192,859 tons. Thereafter through traffic increased to a peak of 294,257 tons in 1845 but had declined to 135,657 tons in 1870. On the other hand total tonnage showed a steady increase to 1,031,284 tons in 1848, 1,142,450 in 1858 and 1,404,012 in 1868.

The end of the Grand Junction's carrying business came in a dramatic way when early on the morning of 2 October 1874 a fleet of six of the company's boats were on the Regent's Canal on their way from City Road Basin to Nottingham. They were being towed by the steamer *Ready*, and on one of the towed boats, *Tilbury*, there were five tons of gunpowder and several barrels of petroleum amongst the cargo. As the procession was passing under Macclesfield bridge *Tilbury* blew up, killing her crew of three outright. The *Limehouse* immediately behind her was sunk and the *Dee* in front badly damaged and her steerer injured. The bridge simply disappeared, and a large number of houses nearby were severely damaged, although by luck this part of the canal is in a small cutting which somewhat reduced the effects of the blast. The cause of the accident was the ignition by a lamp, or the cabin fire, of petroleum vapour.[24] The canal itself was completely blocked and not reopened until the afternoon of 6 October, despite the efforts of 100 men working day and night.

At first the company tried to deny responsibility for the damage, but a court case was decided against it. Eventually over 800 claims were received and nearly £80,000 was paid out in compensation, the company's bankers coming to the rescue with a £40,000 loan, which was finally repaid towards the end of 1877. On top of the carrying losses, which had risen in 1875 owing to higher costs, this disaster made the company decide to give up carrying from 1 July 1876. Much of the trade passed to other carriers, the traffic manager Hughes joining the London & Staffordshire Carrying Co, later part of Fellows Morton & Clayton, which took over most of the Midlands traffic and several boats and steamers. Some of the company's agents got together to form the Midland Counties Carrying Co to take over the trade between London, Leicester, Nottingham, Derby and Sandiacre. This firm hired part of the City Road premises and those at Leicester and Nottingham, and also took over several boats. Other boats and depots were sold off or leased until the only reminder of the carrying days was the preference stock. For some time the company had pursued a policy of buying in its preference shares for cancellation and by June 1863 the amount outstanding was reduced to £100,000. Later this was reduced still further to £93,700.

To take its mind away from the railway challenge the company had to contend with one trying incident at Rickmansworth in 1838. The Lord of the Manor of Rickmansworth, a Mr Dimes, was faced with the manorial responsibility of having to rebuild Batchworth bridge, which carried the Pinner and Harrow turnpike. This was likely to cost a substantial sum of money, but Dimes discovered he had rights to some copyhold land over which the canal had been built. The land had been purchased from Joseph Skidmore and at the time Skidmore had indemnified the company to the extent of the purchase price against all claims. Copyhold land was held by a tenant during his lifetime, but on his death it could revert to the Lord of the Manor.

Skidmore died in 1835 and as no relative claimed the land Dimes had stepped in and in 1836 had brought an action in Hertford Assizes to eject the company from the land. The action failed but Dimes appealed. The appeal was heard on 7 June 1838 and the previous decision was reversed, whereupon Dimes erected a bar across the canal and also across the turnpike road. The company managed to obtain an injunction on 18 June to restrain Dimes from stopping the canal trade for the next five days. Meetings were then held at which Dimes claimed his interest in the land was worth £10,000 but that he would be prepared to accept half this sum if it was paid immediately. The company made an offer of over £3,560, which was calculated at 9½ years purchase of Dimes' proportionate share of the canal's net profit. Dimes attended another meeting with the company on 23 June at which he turned down the company's offer, but in the meantime the company had managed to trace Skidmore's son and heir, who, its legal advisers claimed, Dimes would have to admit as tenant upon a reasonable fine being paid. The company thereupon offered to pay this fine, calculated at £1,500. As expected Dimes refused and the matter again went to court and in November 1846 the Vice-Chancellor gave his judgement that Dimes would have to admit Skidmore's son as tenant. But it was not until 1852 that the incident was settled and the company could enjoy the uninterrupted use of its canal.

One thing the railways did not affect was the repairs to Blisworth tunnel that continued non-stop. In 1849 a length of brickwork was found to be badly distorted and on John Lake's suggestion iron ribs, or struts, were installed early in October until proper repairs could be carried out. The ribs remained in place until 1854. Thereafter there were few years when major works were not needed. In 1864 nearly 20yd of invert had to be replaced and two dams put into the tunnel so that repairs could be carried out, and so the struggle went on.

When the tunnel was opened all traffic on the canal was horse-drawn and the boats had to be shafted or legged through, whilst the horses were walked over the top. Legging consisted of walk-the boats through, with two of the crew lying at the ends of two planks fixed across the bows of the boat, and pushing with their feet against the tunnel walls. At Blisworth where the traffic was heavy there were gangs of professional leggers stationed one at each end. They were issued with a brass armlet and were known as 'registered leggers'. The men only handled traffic one way; the Blisworth men worked southbound and the Stoke men north-bound boats, and four men from each gang were on duty at night.[25] These gangs were employed by the company and received 18d (7½p) per trip. Huts were provided at each end of the tunnel where the men waited for the boats; one was next to the Boat inn at Stoke Bruerne and the other opposite Blisworth mill. The nearby bridge at Blisworth is still called Candle bridge, for the boatmen used to buy tallow dips there to light them through the tunnel. The registered leggers were instituted in 1827; before that system was on a casual basis and boatmen were often terrorised to force them to employ leggers.

In July 1844 an inquiry was made into the possibility of using a steam tug boat, similar to that in use at Islington tunnel on the Regent's Canal, at both Blisworth and Braunston but the idea came to nothing. In July 1870 the question of superseding the legging system came up again and the engineer was told to investigate a wire rope haulage system for both tunnels. His report was favourable and on 20 July 1870 he was authorised to instal it at

Braunston. The work did not take long, being finished in October; it was decided to give it a fair trial before installing the same system at Blisworth. This caution was justified, for at the end of November the system proved a failure, mainly because of the excessive friction caused by the curves in the tunnel and the great strain on the rope.

In April 1871 a steam tug was put to work at Braunston with a charge of 1s 6d (7½p) each way for boats with cargoes of 25 tons and over, 1s 3d (6p) for boats carrying less than 25 tons and 1s (5p) for empty boats. The leggers were disbanded and the company paid a pension of 5s (25p) per week to three of them including one man, then 75 years old, who had been at the tunnel for 44 years and who must have been one of the original leggers when the registered system was first started. The wire rope was carried along both walls of the tunnel on a series of pulleys. The engine house for the steam engine that drove the rope was at the south end of the tunnel and at the north end the wire passed round a large pulley and then back down the other side of the tunnel. A charge of 1s (5p) was made for the use of the wire whilst the system was working. Early in 1872 the company accepted an offer of £50 for some of the pulleys and wire rope that had been used.

Meanwhile tugs had been put on at Blisworth in February 1871, seventeen leggers being paid off and five others found other work. These boats worked to a regular timetable. But the appearance of steam-driven craft gave rise to ventilation problems, particularly at the long Blisworth tunnel. This was high-lighted by an accident in September 1861 when two men were suffocated during the passage of a steam boat through the tunnel.[26] Immediate steps were taken to improve the ventilation and within a week Jesse Cherry had opened out one of the old construction shafts in the middle of the tunnel and negotiations were started with the Duke of Grafton for his permission to reopen two other shafts. There were more complaints in 1864 and the matter was taken up again in June 1881 when another two shafts were opened: seven shafts now act as ventilators.

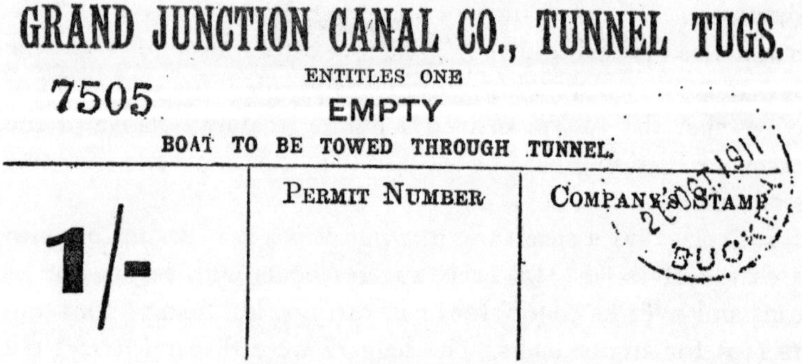

GRAND JUNCTION CANAL CO., TUNNEL TUGS.

ENTITLES ONE

7505   **EMPTY**

BOAT TO BE TOWED THROUGH TUNNEL.

1/- | PERMIT NUMBER | COMPANY'S STAMP

FIGURE 15. Tunnel tug ticket

Another problem brought by steam-driven craft was that a layer of soot built up on the tunnel roof and eventually became so thick that it was essential to remove it. At first a hawthorn bush was tied to the top of a boat and drawn through, but later a special 'brushing' boat was devised. Three wire brushes shaped to the profile of the tunnel were attached to long arms which were hinged centrally on a trestle structure, which in turn was mounted on a dredging boat. The hopper was then towed through the tunnel, the brushes being kept in contact with the roof by men pressing down on the opposite ends of the handles. The brushes were so mounted that the soot dropped down into the hopper. Thereafter the tunnel was swept out regularly by this strange boat.

Throughout the early years of the railway age the company was under the chairmanship of Philip Pleydell Bouverie, until he was succeeded by Sir Francis Bond Head at the beginning of June 1840. For most of his term of office Bouverie also acted as general manager, for which he at one time received a salary of £750. Sir Francis Head also acted as general manager, initially at a salary of £750 but later this was doubled. Sir Francis was replaced by Thomas Grahame in 1847, who in turn was succeeded by George Anderson in 1854. Anderson remained in the chair until 1868 when the Hon Robert Howe Brown took over until his death in 1888.

The office of clerk was filled by Richard Sale until his death in June 1845, after nearly a lifetime spent in the service of the Grand Junction. He was replaced by Thomas Chrimes at a salary of £400, but Chrimes had to resign in October 1845 owing to ill health. To fill the gap Charles Rogers, who had been appointed the company's accountant in December 1842 when George Jackson retired, became acting clerk and he seems to have done so well that his appointment was made permanent in 1847. In the early days the clerk was mainly concerned with legal matters, but as time went on more and more of the day to day management of the canal fell upon his shoulders. Rogers retired in 1869 and was elected to the select committee, his place being taken by Charles Mercer. Mercer died in October 1886 and was succeeded by his son, Charles W. Mercer, who resigned in 1891 following investigations into deficiencies in the accounts.

On the engineering side John Holland was dismissed as southern district engineer in December 1838 when it was found he was getting suppliers of materials to give false invoices and receipts for money they had not received, and for which he was then getting the company to reimburse him. His place was taken at first by John Lake but in January 1841 the southern district was extended northwards to Berkhamsted and William Brown was appointed, whilst John Lake was transferred to the middle district whose boundaries were amended to cover from Berkhamsted to Fenny Stratford. The middle district had had no permanent engineer since 1835 when Thomas Lake was transferred to the northern district. In March 1839 Thomas Armstrong had been appointed but he was dismissed in June of that year and in July the district had been temporarily divided, William Haynes being appointed to take charge of the section from Hunton Bridge to Marsworth and Thomas Lake covering from Marsworth to Leighton Buzzard in addition to the northern district.

In January 1841 the northern district was divided into two sections, from Fenny Stratford to the bottom of Buckby locks with Haynes in charge, and from Buckby to Braunston with Thomas Lake in charge. As senior engineer Thomas Lake also acted as consultant for the whole length of the canal. Brown was sacked in July 1843 and shortly afterwards John Lake took over the southern as well as the middle district. In the north Jesse Cherry took over from Thomas Lake and William Haynes in a reunited northern district. John Lake died in 1864 and the company took the chance to appoint an engineer for the whole canal. This was Hubert Thomas, who started with a salary of £300, but which was soon increased, and by 1885 had reached £1,000. Hubert Thomas served as engineer until 1891, when he became clerk to the company, his son Gordon becoming engineer. It was during the reign of the two Thomases that there were some important developments on the Grand Junction.

CHAPTER 8

The Leicester Line

THE river Trent has been used for transport from the earliest times. For many years Nottingham was the head of navigation, the river, with its outlet to the sea via the river Humber, being the main artery for the trade of the East Midlands. After the Civil War there was a general period of expansion to the country's navigable river network and on the Trent the navigation had been extended to Burton, and the Derwent made navigable to Derby by the early 1720s. With these extensions it was not unnatural that thoughts should turn towards trying to make the river Soar, an important tributary that passed through Leicester and Lough-borough on its way northwards to join the Trent, navigable for boats and barges. As early as 1634 Letters Patent had been granted by Charles I for the Soar to be made navigable to Leicester, but the attempt failed, as did several others. Not until 1775, following initiative from the town of Loughborough, was a smaller scheme put forward for canalising the Soar for 9 miles from its junction with the Trent up to the town to help in opening up local trade. An Act[1] was obtained in April 1776 and the work completed throughout in two years, although parts of the river were passable by the middle of 1777. The undertaking was soon highly profitable. A first dividend of 5 per cent was paid in 1780, ten years later it had risen to 20 per cent, by 1800 it was over 60 per cent and a peak of over 150 per cent was reached in the late 1820s.

Soon after work on the Loughborough Navigation had started a complementary scheme was put forward for a canal to run up the Erewash valley north from the Trent to Langley Mill. This was designed to provide an outlet for the collieries in the area whose produce could then pass down the Erewash Canal, across the Trent and up the Soar to Loughborough, whence road transport could distribute the coal to Leicester and the surrounding area.[2] The proposal won much support[3] and the canal was opened in 1779. Like the Loughborough Navigation the Erewash was soon paying a good dividend on its capital.

But despite the success of these two navigations it was not until 1791 that an Act[4] was obtained for extending the Soar navigation southwards from Loughborough nearly 16 miles to Leicester. This was the culmination of several previous attempts which all foundered, mainly owing to opposition from colliery owners in west Leicestershire and various landowners.[5] The Leicester Navigation was opened formally in October 1794 and a busy trade soon developed, particularly in coals not only from the Derbyshire and Nottinghamshire coalfield, but also from the west Leicestershire coalfield by way of the Forest line, a part-canal part-railway line, which linked up with the navigation at Loughborough.

With trade growing rapidly on the Loughborough and Leicester Navigations it did not take long before suggestions were being made to extend the navigation further south from Leicester to widen the market for coals and other goods. Market Harborough was sufficiently large to attract attention and early in 1792 a meeting was held in the town to consider the possibility of making a canal from Leicester.[6] This scheme had influential backing from several prominent people of the district and a section of the business community in Leicester, besides attracting much general support, so much so that a more ambitious plan was being considered by the middle of 1792. This was for a further extension from Market Harborough to Northampton to link up with the river Nene and with the Grand Junction Canal by a branch.[7] The initial survey was made by Christopher Staveley and, to start with, the two extensions, from Leicester to Market Harborough and from Market Harborough to Northampton, were in the hands of separate committees with separate subscription lists.

In the summer of 1792 William Jessop was appointed engineer, with John Varley to carry out detailed surveys. Varley at first recommended a junction with the Grand Junction at Gayton and a branch to Northampton and the Nene, but the Grand Junction got in first with its own branch from Gayton to the Nene, and so the proposed junction of the two canals was amended to a point on the Grand Junction's branch near Northampton. There was also a tentative suggestion for a further extension beyond Northampton to link up with the river Lee at Hertford and connecting with the river Great Ouse at Bedford,[8] but this idea was passed over in favour of using the Grand Junction's line for the through route to London. There seems to have been little opposition and an Act[9] for the Leicestershire and Northamptonshire Union Canal as it was called, or the Old Union Canal as it was more popularly referred to later, was obtained on 30 April 1793, the same day as the Grand Junction's Act was passed.

This Act authorised making the river Soar navigable from West Bridge in Leicester upstream to Aylestone and a canal from there to the Grand Junction at Hardingstone, and having a level junction with the river Nene near Northampton. The main line was almost 44 miles long and there was to be a branch of nearly 4 miles long from Lubenham to Market Harborough. Apart from a series of locks out of the Soar valley and down again into the Nene valley the main engineering works were four tunnels: Saddington 880yd, Foxton 1,056yd, Kelmarsh 990yd and Great Oxendon 286yd. The Act authorised the raising of £200,000 in £100 shares, with a further £100,000 should it be needed.

Work started at the Leicester end with Varley and Staveley in charge, and on 28 October 1794 the canal was opened to Blaby,[10] just over 5 miles from Leicester through eight locks. By March of the following year Kilby, a further 3 miles through four locks, had been reached. But things were not going well for the company. It was finding it difficult to raise funds fast enough and was having many other problems to contend with, such as labour disputes. Indeed, in October 1795, it was decided to do no work south of Gumley. Contracts for Saddington tunnel were let in

July 1795, the work being completed in February 1797, though not
without some trouble when it was discovered the tunnel was
not perfectly straight. Three short sections had to be widened
slightly to permit broad barges to pass through safely. On 7 April
1797 the canal was opened to Debdale wharf near Gumley, a
distance of almost 17 miles through twenty-five locks from
Leicester.[11] There matters rested, although at the end of 1800
a reservoir to supply the canal with water was completed at
Saddington.

It was not until 1799 that James Barnes was borrowed from the
Grand Junction to make recommendations for linking the unfinished Old Union Canal to the Grand Junction at Braunston.
Nothing came of this, but in 1802 Barnes made another survey for
a line through Welford and Crick to Norton on the Braunston
summit of the Grand Junction. His estimate for the line, with a
branch to Market Harborough, was almost £147,000. Thomas
Telford, called in to advise on Barnes' route, recommended a
much more roundabout line though with less locks by using part
of the original line through Market Harborough, but still linking
with the Grand Junction at Norton. Telford's estimate was over
£228,000 and even this did not include a proposed branch to
Rushton, about 3 miles north of Kettering.[12] Still nothing was
done, but in 1804 the company decided to seek Parliamentary
powers to vary the line between Gumley and Market Harborough,
principally to avoid the long tunnel at Foxton. A second Act was
obtained in June 1805.[13] Even then it was over four years before
the 6¾ mile level extension to Market Harborough, costing over
£40,000, was opened with considerable ceremony on 13 October
1809.[14] The company had made a half-hearted attempt in 1807 to
investigate the possibility of a connection with the Grand Junction but finally, in May 1808, the decision was taken to terminate
at Market Harborough.

In the meantime the initiative had been taken by the Grand
Junction, who had prompted a group of promoters to get Telford
and Barnes to do another survey. The Old Union company was
happy to support this move, at least in spirit. It really got under

way at a meeting in London in June 1808. Benjamin Bevan was
called in as surveyor, and his first task was to sift through the
various plans and select the best route. Apart from the lines
suggested by Telford and Barnes there was also a plan for a canal
from near Blaby to Cosford, near Rugby, on the Oxford. By the
end of 1808 Bevan favoured a route that followed Barnes' line
from Foxton through Welford to Crick, but then avoided a tunnel
by linking up with the Oxford at Braunston.[15] It is certain that
this connection with the Oxford did not suit the Grand Junction
at all and finally in May 1809 a line with a tunnel at Crick and
linking up with the Grand Junction at Norton was adopted. This
was virtually the same route that Barnes had put forward in 1802.
The estimate was £205,000.

The Grand Junction, which had been largely responsible for
getting the new project off the ground, was very strong in its
support, not only for the connection the new canal would give
with the Soar, the Trent and other waterways, but also in the
hope of a shorter canal route to Manchester by using the Erewash,
the Cromford and a proposed new canal across the Peak to link up
with the Peak Forest Canal. This latter objective aroused the
wrath of the Bridgewater and Trent & Mersey interests, who
retaliated by lodging petitions against the Bill for the Grand Union
Canal, as the new canal was called. They were only placated when
the Grand Junction agreed to withdraw its support for the Peak
canal project. Other opposition came from the Oxford company,
which was eventually indemnified against the loss of trade; from
Northampton and the river Nene Commissioners who were
pressing the Grand Junction to build the branch from Gayton to
Northampton and who used this opportunity to force con-
cessions from the company; and from Aylesbury which was also
trying to get its branch canal built and made good use of this
chance to get what it wanted from the Grand Junction. The
Grand Union Act[16] eventually received the Royal Assent on 24
May 1810, and authorised the raising of £245,000 in shares of
£100 or £50, with a further £50,000 if needed.

As in the case of the Old Union, construction of the new canal began from the north at Foxton, where there was a flight of ten locks in two staircases of five, lifting the canal 75ft up to its 20 mile long summit pound. By June 1812 the canal from the top of the locks was open a distance of about 5 miles to the cutting at the north end of Husbands Bosworth tunnel.[17] On 1 October Foxton locks were finished and part of the line south from Husbands Bosworth was open. Eight shafts were used during the construction of the tunnel, which is 1,170yd long, the brickwork being completed on 29 April 1813. On 25 May 1813 the deep cutting to the south of the tunnel was finished and the canal opened to Stanford, about 10 miles from Foxton, together with the first mile of the Welford branch to Welford mill.[18]

In the meantime Bevan had found quicksands and other poor strata on the line of the proposed 1,000yd long tunnel at Crick and in 1812 the original line was abandoned. The revised route ran to the east of Crick village, which involved a longer tunnel of 1,528yd, but an overall shortening of the canal by over 700yd. There was originally to have been a third tunnel, about a quarter of a mile long, with a deep cutting at Watford above the locks, but this was avoided in October 1813 by diverting through Watford park, the company paying the landowner £2,000 in compensation, excluding the cost of the land. At Watford the descent from the summit to the level of the Grand Junction was made by seven locks in a group, of which four were in a staircase. The entire main line, 23⅛ miles long with seventeen locks, was opened on 9 August 1814[19] and then early in 1815 Welford lock was completed and the short branch of 1⅝ miles opened throughout to Welford wharf. This branch also served as a feeder to supply the canal with water from reservoirs on Naseby Wolds.

The Grand Union locks were built narrow, thus breaking the chain of wide locks between London, the East Midlands and the North East. At the time the Grand Junction was opposed to barges and wide boats passing through its long Blisworth tunnel, since this would mean that a system of one-way traffic would have to be introduced and delays to the trade would be severe. In any case most of the carriers who were likely to use the new through route had forecast that narrow boats would be used. So the decision was taken to build narrow locks, with a considerable saving in cost and water consumption, but it was a decision that was to give rise to much controversy later. However, bridges and tunnels were built to a 14ft gauge so that barges could have used them if the locks had permitted.

The Old Union had a moderately successful existence to start with. A maiden dividend was paid in 1812, with steady payments being made thereafter, rising to a peak of 6 per cent in 1837. A decline then set in, with a particularly sharp drop in 1851 and by 1855 the dividend was down to 2⅛ per cent, and to ½ per cent by 1871. The Grand Union was in a much more parlous state. Unlike the Old Union, which had a fair amount of local business, the Grand Union depended almost entirely on through trade for its revenue and was thus very much at the mercy of other companies on the route. It also had a large burden of debt in its early days, which was not finally paid off until 1836. A first dividend of 1 per cent was paid in 1827; this did not rise until 1840 and then only to 1¾ per cent. As with the Old Union a decline set in, with the dividend down to ½ per cent by 1865 and to 1s per cent in 1885. From 1863 the Grand Union entered into an informal arrangement with the Old Union and thereafter the two concerns were worked virtually as a single company. Throughout their existences both Union companies seem to have enjoyed cordial relations with the Grand Junction, which at one time had a substantial share holding in the Grand Union company. Certainly the companies were usually ready to co-operate over toll reductions, without the frustrating negotiations that accompanied similar approaches to the Oxford. In 1865 the Grand Junction did have a row with the Grand Union over tolls paid by its Carrying Establishment, but this was far from typical.

In 1881 Leicester Corporation obtained an Improvement Act which enabled them to widen and straighten the river Soar through the city to relieve flooding. The first two locks at Castle mill and Swan's mill on the Old Union were demolished and replaced by a new lock roughly half a mile to the south in about 1888. The entire project was completed by the spring of 1890, the new cut being opened in February.

Towards the end of the 1880s, by which time both Union canals were in a bad state, the Grand Junction, perhaps prompted by Fellows Morton & Clayton, the principal carriers on the Leicester line, inspected both canals and approached the two companies in an effort to increase the through traffic. The companies replied saying they were prepared to sell, whereupon the Grand Junction offered £5,000. This was turned down, the companies countering with a request for £25,000, since they considered they had a considerable asset in their water supplies. This was too much for the Grand Junction and the matter was dropped for the time being.

Then in February 1893 the Grand Union's engineer suggested that matters would improve if the carriers, particularly Fellows Morton & Clayton, showed more enterprise in trying to attract trade. A meeting followed at which Mr Fellows pointed out that trading was almost impossible at present but that his company would put on large steamers, which could compete with other forms of transport, if both canals were thoroughly dredged and the locks at Watford and Foxton widened. After this meeting Fellows suggested to the Grand Junction that it should buy out the two Union companies and modernise the Leicester line, and not long afterwards a figure of £20,000 was quoted by the two companies. The Grand Junction then authorised Fellows to go ahead, acting as its agent, and on 12 July 1893 he reported that he had obtained the Grand Union for £10,500 and the Old Union for £6,500, with a £250 payment as compensation to their joint clerk. Later the total price was increased by £150 to include winding up costs. The companies held winding up meetings on 16 November and the transfer Act[20] was passed in 1894, the actual purchase taking place on 29 September.

The Grand Junction's first act with its new acquisitions was to put in hand a comprehensive dredging programme which continued sporadically for the next ten years. This was not all, for the company then went on to negotiate with the Leicester and

The Northampton
branch: (*left*) draw-
bridge at Rothers-
thorpe locks; (*below*)
the distinctive design of
lock house

Page 192   Working boats: (above) a cluster at Stoke Bruerne;
(below) descending Hanwell locks

Loughborough Navigations and the Erewash company for a new low through toll. An agreement was reached with the Grand Junction giving a guarantee to make up to £350 for the Leicester, £200 for the Loughborough and £150 for the Erewash if the through tolls did not reach these minimum figures each year. This gave the Grand Junction virtual control, as far as toll rates were concerned, of the waterways line from the Nottingham-shire and Derbyshire coalfield to London. In addition, the Grand Junction secured an option to purchase the three navigations early in 1897; the Leicester for £38,075, the Loughborough for £26,250 and the Erewash for £21,000. At the same time the company, doubtless spurred on by suggestions from Fellows Morton & Clayton, was considering plans to widen the Watford and Foxton flights of locks. The carriers were sure that with wide boats in operation they could reduce their costs and thus increase their traffic between London, Leicester, Nottingham and Derby.

Certainly if traffic on the Leicester line was to be developed, something had to be done. In 1850 some 125,000 tons of Derby-shire coal had reached the Grand Junction, but this had declined to 73,000 tons in 1855 and to a mere 4,700 tons by 1894. This drop reflected the intense railway competition for this lucrative traffic, particularly from the Midland Railway.

There was considerable support for the widening proposals and in July 1896 the company agreed in principle to the construc-tion of an inclined plane lift at Foxton to supersede the ten narrow locks there and be capable of taking a 70 ton barge or a pair of narrow boats. A decision on the Watford locks was deferred, but Fellows Morton & Clayton agreed to put on extra narrow boats on the Leicester line while the plane was being built. The development of the plane was entrusted to Gordon Thomas, who had introduced the idea to the company in the first place, and with the help of his brother James he constructed a large scale model at Bulbourne works to test the feasibility of the design. The model comprised two watertight tanks, resting level on carriages which ran on rails up and down the incline, counter-balancing one another. In November 1896 a large party of experts

M

visited the Thomas' trial installation, which was worked by a portable steam engine, and shortly afterwards the company invited tenders for the full-scale work at Foxton. A year later the tender of J. & H. Gwynne & Co of Hammersmith for the supply and erection of the steelwork for £14,130 was accepted. Construction work started early in 1898, the company carrying out by direct labour the earthworks for the plane itself, the two canal arms and all the brickwork, with from 200 to 300 men being employed at the height of the activity. The plane was completed in June 1900 and opened to traffic on 10 July, the first boat to pass through being the steam boat *Gadfly*, the inspection launch of T. W. Millner, the northern district engineer. The first working boat through was reported to have been Fellows Morton & Clayton's steamer *Phoenix*.

The installation at Foxton comprised two parallel sloping planes with a tank running sideways on each. The tanks were 8oft in length, 15ft wide and 5ft deep inside and weighed about 250 tons, each being supported on eight pairs of wheels running on rails arranged into four pairs. As the boats were carried afloat in the tanks the weight was the same, whether or not they were loaded. The two tanks counterbalanced each other, being linked by a wire balance rope secured to the centre on each side of the tank and passing round pulleys at the top and bottom of the planes, thus forming a continuous circle, and by two 7in steel wire haulage ropes attached to the ends of the tank and passing round two winding drums at the top in the engine house. The ropes were carried on rollers set into the face of the planes. To permit staggered berths at top and bottom the northernmost plane was set back somewhat. At the bottom the tanks were submerged and the boats merely floated in or out, but to compensate for the loss of counter-balancing weight as the descending tank submerged the gradient of the rails at the top of the incline was reduced by making them curve over. To keep the tanks perfectly level, however, an additional pair of leading wheels on the short upper leg came into operation on short sections of track, which continued the gradient and prevented the tanks from tilting.

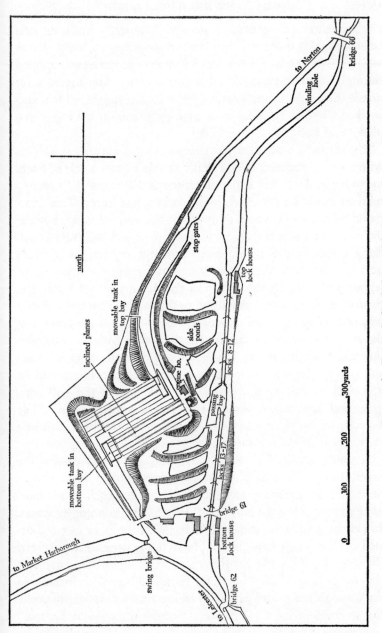

FIGURE 16. Foxton inclined plane and locks

Guillotine gates were fitted at each end of the tanks and at the two ends of canal at the top of the plane; when at the top, the tank was sealed to the end of the canal by hydraulic pressure supplied through buffer stops at the other end. The winding drums were driven through worm gearing by a steam engine which also worked a hydraulic pump to operate the buffers at the top of the planes and the guillotine gates.[21]

The plane overcame the 75ft change of level and was 307ft long with a 1 in 4 gradient. Officially it was able to pass a pair of boats in twelve minutes, but in practice it seems that times of about five minutes could be achieved for boats in a real hurry. This compared with about seventy minutes for the narrow locks, but the main benefit was in the enormous amount of lockage water saved. For the first six months expenses came out at £1 4s 6d (£1.22½) per day, but later these rose somewhat, the main items being labour and coal. In the long run the plane was not a success. Primarily, there were subsidence problems with the rails giving way and being distorted under the great weight of the tanks, but the main reason for its failure was that traffic over the Leicester line was too irregular to justify the engine being kept in steam and paying the staff of three—one in the engine house and an attendant at the top and the bottom to operate the guillotine gates and supervise boats entering and leaving the tanks. The capacity of the plane was about 3,000 tons in each direction in a twelve-hour shift, but traffic never approached these figures.

A similar inclined plane was contemplated for by-passing the seven narrow locks at Watford, but even before Foxton was in operation the company seems to have decided against this, perhaps on account of the initial cost and probable running expenses. In February 1900 the widening of the Watford locks was authorised at a cost of £17,000, but in March it was decided to postpone the work until the Foxton plane was working satisfactorily. But the company was losing heart, for there had been little increase in the through traffic and payments had to be made regularly under the guarantees to the Leicester, Loughborough and Erewash companies. As a result, in 1900 the Grand Junction allowed its options to purchase to lapse and although in the following year the three navigations offered themselves to the Grand Junction for £50,000 the company declined, pointing out that it had already spent a large sum for no return and that it was most disappointed at having to give up a scheme aimed at developing the coal traffic. In 1902 the company again turned down a suggestion that it should buy the three navigations, obviously fearing that they would become a burden such as the two Union canals were proving to be. The widening experiment finished when, between November 1901 and February 1902, the Watford flight of locks was rebuilt as a narrow flight at a cost of nearly £10,000. In June 1902 the company was able to announce that the extensive dredging programme from Norton to Leicester was virtually complete.

Gordon Thomas, in his evidence to the Royal Commission on Canals and Waterways, claimed that the through trade had failed to develop owing to the poor state of both the Cromford Canal, owned by the Midland Railway, and the Erewash Canal; the disuse of the Nutbrook Canal and the high tolls on the Nottingham Canal, controlled by the Great Northern Railway. It certainly seems that the Foxton plane, apart from the subsiding rails, worked satisfactorily, but it was only a matter of time before economics dictated that the plane should be closed. In November 1908 it was decided to reinstate the ten locks at Foxton, primarily to pass traffic at night when the plane was not working, and this was done during 1909. On 26 October 1910 it was announced that the working of the plane would be discontinued after a fortnight and all traffic was to use the locks. Occasional use was made of the plane after November 1910, certainly at times in 1912 and possibly later still. In 1914, however, there was some dismantling and the plane was completely taken down between 1924 and 1926. Much of the material was re-used by the company, the remainder being sold for scrap in 1928 for £250.[22] With the passage of time the remains are fast disappearing. The plane itself has become almost completely overgrown, but the foundations of the engine house can still be traced. The short branch to the Old Union at the bottom of the plane is now used for moorings but the branch at the top is completely overgrown.

This was the end of the Grand Junction's attempt to improve the Leicester line. The two canals had cost £19,123 and by 1928 almost £78,700[23] had been spent on reinstating the works, including the plane which had cost almost £40,000. To finance the works money had been raised on 4 per cent debentures, but there had been little return with only a marginal increase in traffic. So the Leicester line venture proved an expensive excursion for the company.

CHAPTER 9

The End of an Era

THE attempt to improve the Leicester line at the end of the nineteenth century was not the only expansion made by the Grand Junction at the time. Another important scheme, completed a few years earlier, had been the building of the Slough branch canal.

In February 1878 Hubert Thomas had written to his chairman:

> Referring to the conversation I had with you respecting constructing a Canal from Bulls Bridge into the Slough District with a view of opening up new brickfields for supply of the London Market. I have no doubt such a scheme could be cheaply constructed and would offer a large source of revenue to the Company. . . .[1]

Thomas was authorised to take preliminary levels and work out the probable cost of building such a branch. In July the company's solicitors were told to apply for Parliamentary powers to build it. A draft Bill had been drawn up by the end of October, which was approved by the shareholders at a special meeting in January 1879 at which Thomas was able to report that his detailed surveys were complete and his estimate for the cost was £70,550. Opposition to the Bill came from the Duke of Northumberland, who was concerned about the effect of the new branch on the river Colne water supplies, and from the Regent's Canal Co, anxious about any adverse effect upon the water supplies for the Long Level. Negotiations and the insertion of protective clauses in the Act resulted in the withdrawal of this opposition. Other opponents were the Great Western Railway Company, with part of whose line the new branch was to run parallel, and from landowners in the Langley area. Notwithstanding, the Bill passed through the House of Lords committee on 26 March and went on to the Commons. Here the committee hearing started on 3 July and after four days it was passed, although the company had to agree to terminate the branch at the Stoke Poges road in Slough rather than to continue further west as had been planned. This was to avoid interference with land belonging to Eton College and the Duke of Leeds. The Act[2] received the Royal Assent on 21 July 1879.

The rest of 1879 was spent in getting materials prepared for the work and finalising the detailed drawings. Meanwhile a sub-committee was formed to superintend the building of the branch and it was decided to raise the funds required by mortgage. Construction work started in earnest at the beginning of 1880, mainly at the eastern end where most of the heaviest works were concentrated. In the course of the first 1,300yd there were three aqueducts; over Fray's river, the Colne and Colne Brook. Much of the canal here was on a substantial embankment, but at Iver a deep and lengthy cutting was required, whilst nearer Langley more heavy cutting and embanking works were needed. About the middle of 1881, when work on the eastern section was progressing well, it was possible to divert some of the labour force to the Slough end, where the works were comparatively easy. On 1 December 1881 Thomas, accompanied by other company officers, navigated the branch from the Iver road bridge to the junction with the main line at Cowley Peachey in a steam launch and the party inspected the rest of the works on the same day. The cutting at Iver, which required an outlay of over £10,000 in labourers' wages alone during the fifteen months it was being excavated,[3] was completed about April 1882 and the canal was filled with water and opened as far as Langley by the end of May. Thereafter, progress to Slough was steady and on 4 December 1882 Thomas was able to report that the branch was open throughout to traffic.[4]

Its opening had one unlooked for result; it sparked off a long dispute with the Regent's company about water supplies which dragged on for several years. But on the credit side the branch gave a big boost to the brickmaking industry and many wharves were established, particularly in the Iver and Langley areas. Alongside the brickworks, sand and gravel extraction was developed and this industry, too, made considerable use of the canal and indeed soon became the largest user, particularly in later years when the supplies of brick earth started to run out. The tonnages on the branch were substantial; for instance in 1905 192,200 tons were carried, though the tendency thereafter was for a gradual decline, the figure being 122,060 tons in 1915[5] and 103,859 tons in 1927. Tolls yielded £7,614 in 1905 and £3,872 in 1915, and as maintenance costs were low the branch made a useful contribution to the company's finances.

The Slough canal was not the only branch to be developed at the southern end of the system. On the short Rickmansworth branch a basin and wharf were built alongside the branch railway line from Watford about 1871 to provide transhipment facilities, and in 1903 a side lock was built to link up with another section of the river Chess to enable sand and gravel to be extracted from nearby land for carriage away by canal. Several gravel pits in the area were also linked to the main canal to permit the gravel to be transported out by barge.

A veritable network of short branches, or docks, appeared in the Yiewsley and Hayes area mainly to penetrate into brickfields and provide a ready means of transport for both the raw materials and the finished products. The output of bricks from yards along the Slough branch and near the main canal was very substantial and went to supply part of the demand created by the continuing rapid expansion of London at the time. The Otter Dock at Yiewsley was extended in the late 1800s and again in 1913, whilst another dock nearby was extended at the end of 1881 by B. S. Liddall and again at the end of 1913 by Sabey & Co to a total length of over 600yd to link up with some ballast pits. At one time a light railway ran from the end of the dock further into the pits and the 1913 extension was probably over the site of the line to avoid transhipment. Stockley Dock close by was built in August 1904 by S. W. Boyer and was extended to about 350yd in June 1914. Similarly Broad's Dock was lengthened in 1880 and

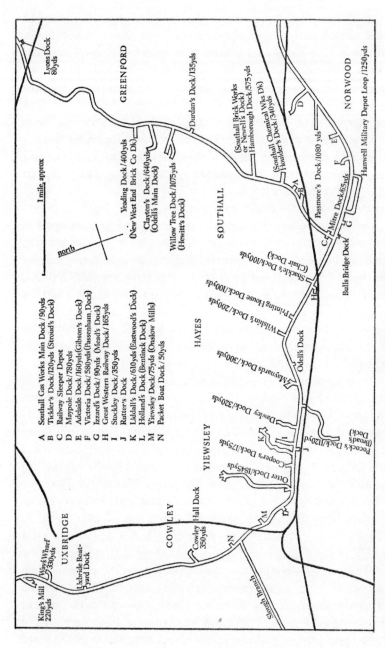

King's Mill 220yds

Way's Wharf 350yds

Uxbridge Boat-yard Dock

UXBRIDGE

Cowley Hall Dock 350yds

COWLEY

Lyons Dock 80yds

GREENFORD

1 mile approx

north

A Southall Gas Works Main Dock / 90yds
B Tickler's Dock / 120yds (Stroud's Dock)
C Railway Sleeper Depot
D Maypole Dock / 780yds
E Adelaide Dock / 160yds (Gibson's Dock)
F Victoria Dock / 580yds (Passenham Dock)
G Izzard's Dock / 90yds (Mead's Dock)
H Great Western Railway Dock / 165yds
I Stockley Dock / 350yds
J Rutter's Dock
K Liddall's Dock / 610yds (Eastwood's Dock)
L Holland's Dock (Bentinck Dock)
M Yiewsley Dock / 75yds (Onslow Mills)
N Packet Boat Dock / 50yds

Yeading Dock / 400yds
(New West End Brick Co Dk)
Clayton's Dock / 640yds (Odell's Main Dock)
Willow Tree Dock / 1075yds (Hewitt's Dock)

Durdan's Dock / 135yds

(Southall Brick Works or Newell's Dock)
Hamborough Dock / 575yds
(Southall Chemical Wks Dk)
Houlder's Dock / 340yds

Passmore's Dock / 1080 yds

Hanwell Military Depot Loop / 1250yds

NORWOOD

Shackle's Dock / 100yds (Chair Dock)

Balls Bridge Dock

Mitre Dock / 65yds

Printing House Dock / 100yds

Wilshin's Dock / 200yds

Maynard's Dock / 300yds

Dawley Dock / 320yds

Pocock's Dock / 120yd (Broad's Dock)

Cooper's Dock / 175yds

Otter Dock / 185yds

Odell's Dock

SOUTHALL

HAYES

YIEWSLEY

Slough Branch

FIGURE 17. London area canal branches

again in 1895 and here again a railway line extended from the branch canal further into the brickfield. In 1895, after several unsuccessful attempts, the Hanwell Military Depot loop line was extended, probably by making the western junction and thus completing the loop. Its total length was 1,500yd. Similarly there was a series of docks off the Paddington branch into the brick-fields at Hayes. As these fields were worked out, so the docks were used to receive rubbish from London boroughs, carried by barge along the Long Level from such places as Marylebone and Paddington.

In December 1913 a completely new dock which ran from just above Norwood top lock for nearly half a mile was opened. This, the Otto Monsted, or Maypole, Dock was built to serve the May-pole margarine works, and reflects its modern construction with its concrete piled banks. It cost £27,670, and a substantial traffic in coconut oil, margarine and other foodstuffs quickly built up on the branch totalling almost 55,000 tons in 1914 and rising to a peak of over 84,500 tons in 1920.[6] Thereafter there was a decline with over 30,000 tons being carried in 1928. The last of the dock extensions was opened in 1922, when a short branch was built at Greenford to serve the factory operated by J. Lyons & Co Ltd. This received its supplies by barge from Brentford and this traffic, too, quickly built up, nearly 10,000 tons being handled in 1922, almost 19,000 tons two years later and over 15,500 tons in 1928.[7]

Certainly the company did all it could to keep its system competitive. This was reflected in the traffic, which was still running at a very high level, despite intense railway competition and the growing impact of road transport. Total tonnage was 1,172,463 in 1888, 1,620,552 in 1898 and 1,794,233 in 1905. By 1925 it had declined to 1,485,346.

The peak traffic was in 1914.[8] In May of that year no less than 34,368½ tons in 2,002 boats passed through lock 45 and in July a peak 46,163¼ tons passed through Norwood lock. The number of craft operating was also substantial. In 1908 6,790 pairs of boats passed through Braunston locks and a further 1,555 single boats, in all carrying about 295,000 tons. In the same year 7,466 pairs and 1,570 singles passed Stoke Bruerne top lock, whilst 3,299 boats passed along the Northampton branch. There was quite a lot of empty running; 2,790 boats passed empty through Braunston northwards and 512 southwards in 1908 and 3,064 northwards and 812 southwards through lock 45.

Year	Tring Summit (lock 45) tons	No of boats	Norwood (lock 90) tons	Foxton (incline/locks) tons
1906	309,270	16,892	355,458	36,309
1908	316,094	18,652	357,565	31,540
1910	343,110	19,498	380,374	40,767
1912	344,907	20,031	350,685	37,258
1914	348,470	20,272	440,516	34,910
1916	281,109	15,267	361,420	15,482
1918	246,318	13,687	331,062	10,385
1920	222,773	12,175	405,945	12,824
1922	255,125	14,941	329,708	11,037
1924	251,957	14,176	366,981	9,917
1926	252,289	13,952	397,792	9,727
1928	313,719	16,819	391,006	9,676

The early 1900s saw several developments in the northern district of the canal. In 1893 the upper part of the north front of Blisworth tunnel on the towpath side started to slip outwards. Wooden struts were erected as a temporary measure but complete reconstruction was the only remedy and this was carried out between December 1902 and October 1903, when the whole of the north portal was rebuilt in blue brickwork at a cost of just over £639.[9] In the early 1920s repairs to the south abutment at Wolverton aqueduct became necessary, the whole of the abutments being refaced, again in blue brickwork, at a cost of £1,700.

There were also problems on the Buckingham branch at Mountmill, some 3½ miles up the arm. At this point the canal runs close to the Great Ouse but at some height above river level. For some time leakages had occurred here, until matters became so bad that in 1919 the company had to drain the affected stretch of canal and concrete the bottom and sides for about 200yd to cure the trouble. Not that this was the only problem with the Buckingham branch. The extreme upper end of the canal in the town itself did not belong to the company and into this section Buckingham Corporation discharged all the town sewage, whilst much refuse from a feeder connecting with the river Great Ouse also accumulated in the canal.[10] Periodically the company cleaned the branch out, on occasions going right into Buckingham, but only legal action at the end of the 1890s, when an injunction was obtained against the Corporation, finally put an end to the trouble.[11]

By this time the damage had been done, for whereas in the early 1890s 2,500 tons of coal and 500 tons of other goods were being brought to Buckingham each year, the final section into the town was in such poor condition that traffic was falling off.[12] In the 1900s about 30 boats each year were still going up to Maids Moreton mill, a mile and a half below Buckingham, with roadstone for the Urban District Council,[13] but there was virtually no traffic to the town itself. Roadstone was still being taken to Leckhampstead wharf for the Rural District Council, and there was a little agricultural traffic and a small amount of trade to Deanshanger. In evidence to the Royal Commission Buckingham Corporation made a firm promise to take 500 tons of stone and 60 tons of coal each year by water if the branch should be re-opened, but the offer was not taken up.

Probably the biggest problem of all at the end of the nineteenth century was on the Tring summit as a result of continuing leakages on the Wendover branch. During the summer of 1897, a particularly dry season, the leakage was found to be so great that it was more than the entire supply coming into the branch at Wendover and was actually drawing water from the main line, making it impossible to maintain a depth of more than 4ft over the Tring summit. On 21 August two sets of stop planks were put in at Little Tring and the intervening space pumped out, thus severing the branch from the main canal.[14] The main line water level immediately improved, whilst on the other side of the dam the level sank notwithstanding the supplies coming in from Wendover. Later this temporary arrangement was made permanent with the construction of a stop lock at Little Tring. The intention was that the branch should be available when there was sufficient water, but the dry weather persisted and the branch remained closed to all intents and purposes except for a short time in 1901 when a few boats navigated up to Buckland. Whilst the branch was closed the Wendover water was run down into Wilstone reservoir.

Several complaints were made about the closure of the branch and in 1903 Lord Rothschild and other landowners approached the Railway & Canal Traffic Commissioners, but these ruled that the Act authorising the making of the branch navigable was permissive and not obligatory, and that the only obligation was to make the branch a feeder. Meanwhile the company pointed out that keeping the branch open would merely endanger the main line. In April 1903 the surviving portion of the branch from the pumping station to the main line, and the main line from the junction to Bulbourne bridge, were drained and repairs carried out to reduce the leakages. On the main line this comprised building brick walls on both sides of the canal and lining the bed with concrete and bitumen sheeting. During all this time Gordon Thomas had been considering what should be done with the closed branch. He put forward three alternatives.[15] The first was to restore the navigation by repairing the asphalt and puddle at a cost of nearly £15,700; the second was to repair the asphalt and puddle and provide brick and concrete side walls between Little Tring and Drayton for over £19,500; and the final scheme was to repair the branch as a water conduit, to cost nearly £4,900, the water level to be permanently lowered.

A variation of the cheapest scheme was finally carried out; in 1904 the bed of the branch between Drayton and Wendover was repaired using clay puddle from the sides of the canal. The water level was lowered and diverted into Wilstone reservoir by the Drayton feeder. The canal between Drayton and the stop lock was then abandoned. This course naturally meant that the bulk of the pumping at Tringford had to be from Wilstone, and as this was low-lying, the costs of pumping to overcome the lift of from

60 to 7½ft were formidable. So much so that Thomas suggested in September 1910 that the Wendover water should be piped along the abandoned stretch of the branch to the pumping station, where a new pump would be installed.[16] The scheme was estimated to cost almost £3,500 and in November the go-ahead was given. But it was found impossible to design a pump to cope satisfactorily with the very variable flow of water from Wendover, ranging from 14 to 42 locks per day, and in April 1911 Thomas proposed that the Wendover water should now pass into a mixing shaft at the pumping station, where it could either be pumped into the summit or passed by gravity to Tringford reservoir. With this amendment Thomas also proposed to reduce the size of the pipeline, the cost now being estimated at almost £2,500. Thomas wanted to scrap the old York engine, which was nearly worn out, and replace it with a new electric pump, whilst the other new pump to draw either from Tringford reservoir or from the Wendover water was also to be electric-powered. Electricity was to be provided by two diesel-driven generators. The total cost of the improvements was about £8,000, but a saving of about 11d per lock was expected in pumping costs on account of the much higher proportion of water to be drawn from the high level Tringford reservoir.

A contract for the supply of the new pumps and electrical equipment at nearly £4,000 was made with Rees Roturbo Ltd in July 1911, but the company carried out all the other works by direct labour, the new pipeline being completed in the early summer of 1912 after 12 months' work.[17] A connection was made to the old heading at Whitehouses so that water could be diverted to Wilstone if required. The water was turned on on 12 June 1912 and the pumps were completed about a year later. Not long afterwards it was decided that the Old engine was also due for renewal, and thenceforward it was only used occasionally to supplement the other pumps. In 1926 William Yates, the engineer, recommended its replacement by new electrically-driven pumps and this proposal was accepted in May. Two Rees Roturbo pumps were supplied and placed at different heights in the pumping well. Both were needed to provide the lift to pump from Wilstone, but either could be used for drawing from the high-level reservoirs. The new plant was formally opened on 19 October 1927, the cost being £4,292, of which £2,344 was for the plant and the rest was for the constructional work, which included the breaking up of the historic beam engine. The new pumps were supplied with electricity from the Borough of Aylesbury power station.

In the summer of 1902 a new engine and pump was installed at Cowroast and the effectiveness of this improved supply of well water was spotlighted in that year when there was acute water shortage at Tring following a series of dry years since 1895, culminating in a severe drought in 1902:

> Between Marsworth and Boxmoor . . . there are 50 pairs of barges waiting for water to float them through the locks. This block is the worst effect of the drought in Hertfordshire and Buckinghamshire. It is causing serious delays in the London supply of all kinds of merchandise—coal and ironware from the Midlands, new corn from some of the arable counties, condensed milk from Aylesbury —and in the Midlands supply of sugar, tea and other commodities in bulk from London. Heroic exertions on the part of the Grand Junction company's engineers and servants do not enable more than 80 to 90 barges a week to pass over the Tring summit, whereas in times of plentiful water 130 pass.[18]

The reservoirs were all virtually empty at the time and it was only the newly-equipped pumping station at Cowroast that enabled the company to keep the summit open at all.

Throughout the 1880s and 1890s the company had held its dividend at a regular 4 per cent, but this fell to 3 per cent in 1903 until 1918, when it started climbing back to 4 per cent again. A decreasing proportion of the company's income came from purely canal operations and it was the revenue obtained from the many properties along the line of the canal and particularly at Paddington that enabled a dividend to be paid. In fact receipts from tolls had been fairly static since the 1870s; for the three years from 1923 to 1925 they averaged £67,553 and from 1926–8, £70,424. But for these periods the income from rents brought in

an average of £41,984 and £42,221 and from the Paddington
estates a further £28,422 and £28,879 respectively. The expenses
of maintaining the canal averaged £41,475 for 1923-5 and
£45,892 for 1926-8, with other expenses at £43,400 and £45,774
respectively.[19] This left about £55,000 available, of which £6,000
was applied to paying the 4 per cent interest on the £150,000
debenture stock in issue and £5,622 the 6 per cent dividend on
the £93,700 of preference stock. Most of the remainder was used
to pay a dividend on the £1,130,000 ordinary capital, which at 4
per cent absorbed £45,200.

But the company did not stint in its efforts to modernise the
canal. At the turn of the century a considerable amount of work
was carried out in the Brentford area, the rural area around the
gauging lock being developed with the building of extensive
wharves and warehouses. The gauging lock itself was duplicated
in 1900 to handle the increased traffic, but plans to provide
another lock near Thames lock were not proceeded with as
Parliamentary powers would have been needed. Coupled with
this work an extensive dredging programme was carried out
throughout the main line and on the Paddington branch, which
originated with the idea of allowing 14ft beam craft to work
through to Leicester. The company invested heavily in new plant
for this work, particularly with new steam dredgers. In 1925
£2,400 was spent on improvements to Walton mill in Aylesbury;
in 1926 a new warehouse was provided at Northampton wharf
costing over £1,250 and in 1927 a new electric crane and improvements to a warehouse at Brentford cost nearly £1,600. In addition
a considerable amount of walling to the canal in the Brentford
area was carried out, to say nothing of the improvements at
Tringford pumping station. On the credit side the value of the
company's property at Paddington was shown in 1927 when a
block of land was sold to the Governors of St Mary's Hospital for
£65,000.[20]

The fairly static toll income was partly explained by the emer-
gence of Fellows Morton & Clayton as by far the largest carriers
on the canal. This firm was already very large when, in 1886, they

N

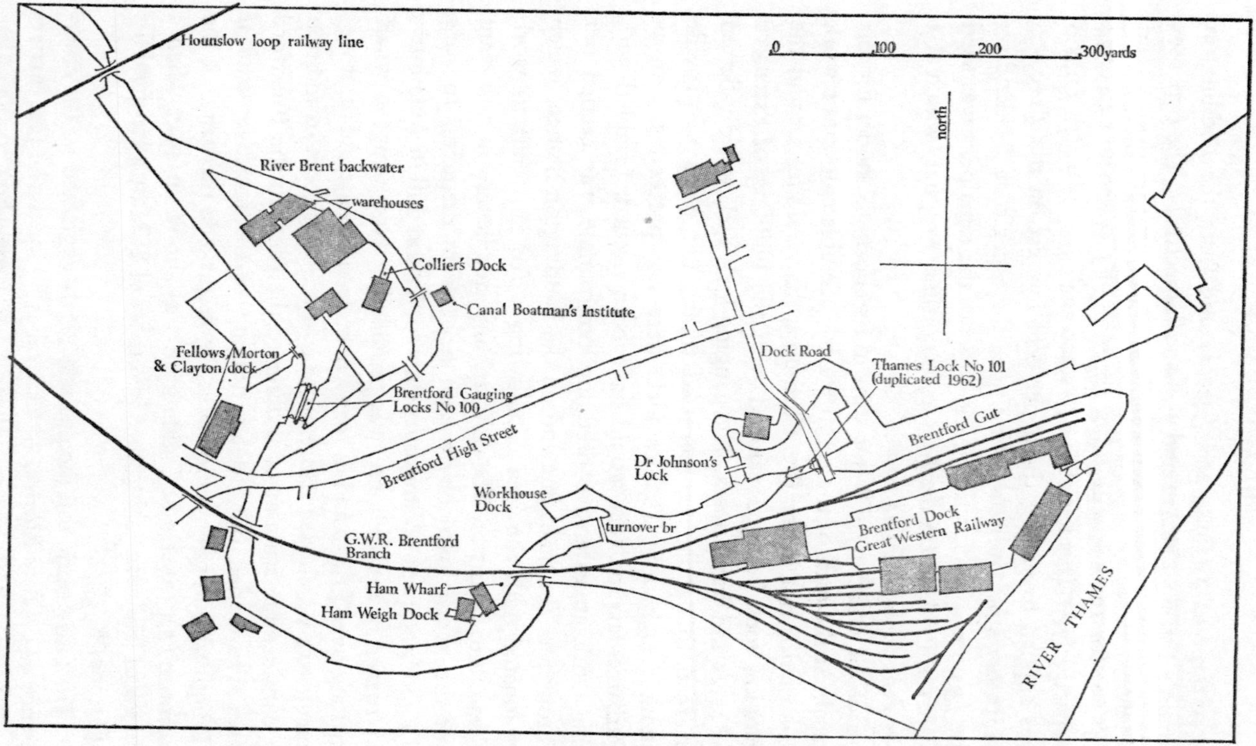

FIGURE 18. Brentford

Hounslow loop railway line

River Brent backwater

warehouses

Colliers Dock

Canal Boatman's Institute

Fellows Morton & Clayton dock

Brentford Gauging Locks No 100

Brentford High Street

Workhouse Dock

turnover br

Dr Johnson's Lock

Dock Road

Thames Lock No 101 (duplicated 1962)

Brentford Cut

G.W.R. Brentford Branch

Ham Wharf

Ham Weigh Dock

Brentford Dock Great Western Railway

RIVER THAMES

north

0   100   200   300 yards

took over the London traffic of the London & Midland Counties Carrying Co, and this enabled them to obtain even better toll rates from the Grand Junction. Indeed in 1905 the through toll between London and Birmingham was 0.158d per ton per mile on average. Of this figure the Grand Junction's share was by far the lowest at fractionally over 0.1d per ton mile, whilst both the Birmingham Canal Navigations and the Oxford Canal Co charged three and a half times this rate.[21] Indeed so serious was the loss of income to the company during a protracted strike among the Fellows Morton & Clayton boatmen in the autumn of 1923 that the Grand Junction's engineer had to take urgent steps to slash maintenance expenditure until trade was back to normal.

In 1914 Rudolph Fane de Salis became chairman of the company, a position he was to retain throughout the remainder of the company's independent life. He succeeded Thomas Tatham, who had in turn taken over from John Stone Wigg in 1898. In 1905 the clerk, Hubert Thomas, who was in poor health, retired and was succeeded by John Bliss, who remained until the end of 1928. Hubert's son, Gordon, remained as the company's engineer until 1916 when he was dismissed for suspected embezzlement and replaced by William Yates.

After World War I the company was not finding life easy and thought was again being given to widening the company's sphere of influence. After the unfortunate experience with the Leicester canals, this time the Birmingham line was studied and in June 1925 a report was made by William Yates on the cost of putting the three canals that made up the route into a proper state of repair. In fact there had been an attempt to take over the Warwick canals soon after the Union canals were acquired, but the enabling Bill had had to be withdrawn from Parliament in June 1895 because of opposition from local authorities on rating grounds. A special committee was set up to investigate a possible purchase or merger and this soon involved the Regent's Canal & Dock Co, which, at the end of 1925, through its chairman W. H. Curtis—also a Grand Junction select committee member— suggested purchasing the Grand Junction except for its interests in the Paddington estates. This proposal made sense to the company as an extension of its own thoughts and throughout 1926 the details were worked out, a provisional agreement being reached in November. Under this agreement the Grand Junction was to go ahead with its original intention of purchasing the three Warwick canals and negotiations were opened with these companies, which were being managed by a joint committee at the time.

Towards the end of 1927 details were finalised—for technical reasons the Regent's purchased the Warwick canals rather than indirectly through the Grand Junction—and Bills were deposited in Parliament in January 1928 to authorise the takeovers. These Acts received the Royal Assent in August 1928 and from 1 January 1929 the combined concern came into being under the name of the Grand Union Canal Co Ltd; a title adopted by the Regent's to signify its wider interests.

The Grand Junction transferred its entire canal assets to the new concern, receiving £285,709 5½ per cent debentures in return, and promoted a further Act of Parliament to convert itself into a limited company. It remained in being as an independent property concern until the end of 1971 when it was taken over for nearly £28 million and is now part of the Amalgamated Investment & Property Co Ltd. The Grand Junction shareholders received Grand Union ordinary shares in the proportion of £67 6s (£67.30) for each £100 of Grand Junction stock.

The Grand Junction held what was, in effect, its final meeting on 12 December 1928 when compensation for the retiring select committee and the retiring clerk was fixed and a portrait of De Salis was presented to him as a parting gift. And so ended the great Grand Junction era. It had lasted for nearly 140 years and had covered one of the most significant periods in the history of this country. From 1929 the Grand Junction carried on as part of a much larger concern, but this story must be told elsewhere.

Notes

NOTES TO CHAPTER 1 (*pages 15–26*)

1. Oxford Canal Committee Minute Book, 11 January 1792.
2. *Northampton Mercury*, 21 July 1792.
3. Ibid, 28 July 1792.
4. Hadfield, Charles. *Canals of the East Midlands*, 2nd ed, 1970.
5. *Northampton Mercury*, 27 October 1792.
6. Ibid, 3 November 1792.
7. Ibid, 8 September 1792.
8. Ibid, 1 December 1792.
9. Ibid, 19 January 1793.
10. *Derby Mercury*, 4 April 1793.
11. *Northampton Mercury*, 20 April 1793.
12. 33 Geo III, c 80.
13. *Northampton Mercury*, 27 April 1793.

NOTES TO CHAPTER 2 (*pages 27–41*)

1. *Northampton Mercury*, 25 May 1793.
2. Lysons, Rev D. *An Historical Account of those Parishes in the County of Middlesex which are not described in the environs of London*, 1800.
3. *Northampton Mercury*, 15 November 1794.
4. Grand Junction Lower District Committee Minute Book, 16 December 1793.
5. Grand Junction General Committee Minute Book, 12 June 1794.
6. 35 Geo III, c 8.
7. Lower District Committee Minute Book, 20 May 1794.
8. *Northampton Mercury*, 25 June 1796.
9. Ibid.
10. *Northampton Mercury*, 17 September 1796.
11. Ibid.
12. General Committee Minute Book, 15 November 1797.
13. Legg, Edward. *Fenny Stratford Bridge, The Lockgate*, vol 2, no 10, January 1968.
14. *Northampton Mercury*, 31 May 1800.
15. General Committee Minute Book, 21 October 1800.

NOTES TO CHAPTER 3 (*pages 42–70*)

1. Probably the same Charles Jones who was employed at Sapperton Tunnel. See Household, Humphrey. *The Thames & Severn Canal*, 1969.
2. Lower District Committee Minutes, 20 May 1794.

3. Lower District Committee Minutes, 3 September 1794.
4. Grand Junction General Assembly Minutes, 1 June 1795.
5. General Assembly Minutes, 7 June 1796.
6. Pitt, William. *General View of the Agriculture of the County of Northampton*, 1809.
7. Hatley, Victor. *The Blisworth Hill Railway*. 1962/3.
8. Ibid.
9. Report to General Assembly, 2 November 1802.
10. Report to General Assembly, 7 June 1803.
11. *Northampton Mercury*, 22 October 1803.
12. Report to General Assembly, 5 June 1804.
13. *Northampton Mercury*, 8 September 1804.
14. Report to General Assembly, 6 November 1804.
15. *Northampton Mercury*, 9 February 1805.
16. Ibid, 16 March 1805.
17. Ibid, 30 March 1805.
18. General Committee Minute Book, 10 December 1799.
19. Report to General Assembly, 8 June 1802.
20. *Oracle*, 13 April 1805.
21. *Northampton Mercury*, 26 April 1805.
22. Ibid, 31 August 1805.
23. Report to General Assembly, 3 June 1806.
24. Hassell, J. *A Tour of the Grand Junction*, 1819.
25. General Committee Minute Book, 14 June 1808.
26. *Northampton Mercury*, 23 July 1808.
27. Ibid, 30 September 1809.
28. Ibid, 26 January 1811.

NOTES TO CHAPTER 4 (*pages* 71–101)

1. 34 Geo III, c 24.
2. 35 Geo III, c 43.
3. 35 Geo III, c 85.
4. General Committee Minute Book, 15 March 1797.
5. *Northampton Mercury*, 9 May 1801.
6. General Assembly Minutes, 3 June 1794.
7. General Assembly Minutes, 7 June 1796.
8. Ibid.
9. General Assembly Minutes, 1 November 1796.
10. *Northampton Mercury*, 18 July 1801.
11. 38 Geo III, c 33.
12. 51 Geo III, c 169.
13. Spencer, Herbert. *London's Canal*, 1961.
14. Ibid.
15. *Northampton Mercury*, 3 May 1800.
16. Ibid, 23 October 1802.
17. Ibid, 27 November 1802.
18. Ibid, 18 February 1803.
19. Ibid, 5 October 1805
20. Ibid, 13 January 1810.
21. Ibid, 6 May 1815.
22. General Committee Minute Book, 17 March 1803.
23. *Northampton Mercury*, 13 September 1806.

24. *Jackson's Oxford Journal*, 2 October 1813.
25. Gibbs, Robert. *History of Aylesbury*, 1883.
26. General Committee Minute Book, 11 May 1815.
27. Rickmansworth Vestry Minutes.
28. Evans, Joan. *The Endless Web*, 1955.
29. Lansberry, H. C. F. *St Albans Canal. Hertfordshire Past & Present*, No 7. 1967.
30. Bedford County Record Office, GA 736/2 & 3.
31. BCRO, GA 736/1.
32. Deposited Plan. Bedford & Grand Junction Canal, 1892.

NOTES TO CHAPTER 5 (*pages* 102–131)

1. 36 Geo III, c 25.
2. Report to General Assembly, 8 June 1802.
3. 41 Geo III, c 71.
4. Report to General Assembly, 8 June 1802.
5. Ibid.
6. Report to General Assembly, 2 November 1802.
7. 43 Geo III, c 8.
8. Grand Junction printed circular notice, 4 June 1804.
9. 45 Geo III, c 68.
10. Lysons, Rev D. *An Historical Account of those Parishes in the County of Middlesex which are not described in the environs of London*, 1800.
11. Report to General Assembly, 8 June 1802.
12. Ibid.
13. Evans, Joan. *The Endless Web*, 1955.
14. Ibid.
15. General Committee Minute Book, 8 May 1817.
16. 58 Geo III, c 16.
17. *The Endless Web*, op cit.
18. Inscription on monument at Rickmansworth Lodge near Batchworth lock.
19. All Grand Junction water tables were measured in locks. A lock being the equivalent of 56,000 gallons.
20. 52 Geo III, c 140.
21. *Northampton Mercury*, 12 November 1808.

NOTES TO CHAPTER 6 (*pages* 132–151)

1. Richardson, Alan. *Water Supplies to Tring Summit. Journal of the Railway & Canal Historical Society*, April 1969.
2. Ibid.
3. McGarey, D. G. *The History of Tringford Pumping Station*, 1946.
4. *Water Supplies to Tring Summit*, op cit.
5. *History of Tringford Pumping Station*, op cit.
6. Ibid.
7. Ibid.
8. The capacity of the Wilstone reservoirs was reduced when the overflow weir was dropped by 12in in November 1936.
9. Thomas, Gordon C. Evidence to Royal Commission on Canals and Inland Waterways, 1908.
10. Ibid.
11. Ibid, 41351.

12. Ibid, 41351.
13. Ibid, 41356.
14. *Water Supplies to Tring Summit*, op cit.
15. Evans, Joan. *The Endless Web*, 1955.
16. *Water Supplies to Tring Summit*, op cit.
17. Report to General Assembly, 7 June 1803.
18. Overflow weir now lowered by 23in making present capacity 5,500 locks.
19. Lower District Committee Minutes, 12 September 1796.
20. *Northampton Mercury*, 31 August 1805
21. Since nationalisation these reservoirs have been connected to the main canal.

NOTES TO CHAPTER 7 (*pages 152–182*)

1. Jeaffreson, J. C. & Pole, W. *The Life of Robert Stephenson*, 1864.
2. LMS Railway Co. *Old Euston*, 1938.
3. Ibid.
4. Rolt, L. T. C. *George & Robert Stephenson*, 1960.
5. *Old Euston*, op cit.
6. *George & Robert Stephenson*, op cit.
7. Ibid.
8. Scrivener, Harry. *A Comprehensive History of the Iron Trade*, 1841.
9. Grand Junction Toll Receipts Book, 1841–75.
10. Ibid.
11. *An Epitome of the Progress of the Trade in Coal to London since 1775.* (1869 edition).
12. Ibid.
13. Bawtree, Maurice. *The City of London Coal Duties*, in *The London Archaeologist*, spring 1969.
14. Bawtree, Maurice. *Stockers House and the London Coal Duties Boundary Marks*, in *Rickmansworth Historian*, autumn 1965.
15. *Aris's Birmingham Gazette*, 12 November 1827.
16. Hadfield, Charles. *Canals of the East Midlands*, 2nd ed, 1970.
17. *London to Birmingham Canal*, in *Lock & Quay*, December 1954.
18. Ibid.
19. *Canals of the East Midlands*, op cit.
20 Toll Receipt Book 1841–75.
21. Ibid.
22. *Case of the Grand Junction Company respecting the Variation of the Warwick & Braunston Canal* (printed leaflet c. February 1796).
23. *Northampton Mercury*, 1 September 1792.
24. *The Regent's Canal Explosion, London 1874* in the *Fire Protection Association Journal*, April 1957.
25. Rolt, L. T. C. *The Inland Waterways of England*, 1950.
26. *Rugby Advertiser*, 14 September 1861.

NOTES TO CHAPTER 8 (*pages 183–198*)

(For a more detailed history of the Leicester line see *The Leicester Line*, by Philip A. Stevens, 1972)

1. 16 Geo III, c 65
2. Hadfield, Charles. *Canals of the East Midlands*, 2nd ed, 1970.
3. An Act (17 Geo III c. 69) was passed on 30 April 1777.

4. 31 Geo III, c 65.
5. *Canals of the East Midlands*, op cit.
6. Union Canal Minute Book, 19 March 1792.
7. *Derby Mercury*, 14 June 1792.
8. *British Chronicle*, 5 December 1792.
9. 33 Geo III, c 98.
10. Union Canal Minute Book, 25 October 1794.
11. Ibid, 19 April 1797.
12. Reports by Jessop and Barnes in the Library of the Institution of Civil Engineers.
13. 45 Geo III, c 71
14. *Northampton Mercury*, 21 October 1809.
15. Ibid, 17 December 1808.
16. 50 Geo III, c 122.
17. *Canals of the East Midlands*, op cit.
18. Ibid.
19. *Derby Mercury*, 18 August 1814.
20. 57 & 58 Vic, c 85 (Royal Assent, 20 July 1894).
21. *Engineering*, 25 January 1800 (illustrated account of the plane).
22. Grand Junction published accounts, 1925–28.
23. Ibid, 1928.

NOTES TO CHAPTER 9 (*pages* 199–212)

1. Select Committee Minute Book, 27 February 1878.
2. 42 & 43 Vic, c 178.
3. Slough Branch Canal Cash Book, 1879–82.
4. Select Committee Minute Book, 5 December 1881.
5. Grand Junction Tonnage Book, 1904–28.
6. Ibid.
7. Ibid.
8. Ibid.
9. Photographic Record Book by T. W. Millner in Waterways Museum.
10. Royal Commission on Canals & Inland Waterways, 1908, 35290 & 41381.
11. Ibid, 41381.
12. Ibid, 35302.
13. Ibid, 35326.
14. Ibid, 41357.
15. Richardson, Alan. 'Water Supplies to Tring Summit,' *Journal of the Railway & Canal Historical Society*, April 1969.
16. McGarey, D. G. *The History of Tringford Pumping Station*, 1946.
17. Ibid.
18. *Daily Mail*, 7 October 1902.
19. Grand Junction Annual Reports, 1923–28.
20. Ibid.
21. Hadfield, Charles. *Canals of the East Midlands*, 2nd ed, 1970.

NOTES TO APPENDIX 3 (*pages* 227–230)

1. *Northampton Mercury*, 26 December 1812.
2. Ibid, 14 August 1813.
3. Ibid, 21 August 1813.
4. 54 Geo III, c 98.

5. *Northampton Mercury*, 26 November 1814.
6. Ibid, 23 November 1816.
7. *Pigot & Co's London & Provincial Directory*, 1823/4.
8. Newport Pagnell Canal Minute Book, 28 August 1845.
9. Minutes of evidence to House of Lords Select Committee on Newport Pagnell Railway Bill.
10. Newport Pagnell Canal Minute Book, 28 January 1846.
11. Ibid, 6 December 1862.
12. Newport Pagnell Railway Act—26 & 27 Vic, c 110—29 June 1863.
13. Newport Pagnell Canal Minute Book, 24 October 1864.

Author's Acknowledgements

DURING the past twelve years whilst I have been delving into the Grand Junction story I have had cause to be grateful to many people who have given me invaluable assistance in piecing this book together. Perhaps firstly I should thank the Archivist at the British Transport Historical Records office at Paddington and his staff who have always been most helpful during my many visits. I am also grateful to the staffs of the Northampton Central Library, the British Museum Newspaper Library, the House of Lords Records Office and the County Archivists for Bedfordshire, Buckinghamshire, Hertfordshire, Greater London and Northamptonshire who have all assisted me in various ways.

I must express my very grateful thanks to Charles Hadlow, former Curator of the Waterways Museum at Stoke Bruerne, who unselfishly put his entire set of notes, built up over many years of active service on the canal, at my disposal and who gave me much other help and encouragement. His successor at the Museum, Richard Hutchings, has also gone out of his way to be helpful to me. My most sincere thanks to Charles Hadfield, who suggested I should write this book and who has given me access to his own notes; to Philip Stevens who read the draft and who helped me with the Leicester line; to Michael Ewans who also read the draft and made many valuable suggestions; to Geoffrey Webb who has been a never-failing source of information over the years; and to my father for his help with the research work and in so many other ways.

Last but not least I would like to thank all the many other people who have assisted me—officers of the British Waterways

Board, members of local history societies, members of the Railway & Canal Historical Society, and other friends, but in particular: E. Bell, A. J. Brawn, H. J. H. Compton, G. Cornwall, G. V. Dyer, V. A. Hatley, E. Legg, K. W. Newham, E. V. Parrott, L. B. Sutherland, A. L. Wood and the late H. C. Weatherhead.

For the illustrations I am indebted to the British Waterways Board for permission to reproduce from the various collections now housed at the Waterways Museum at Stoke Bruerne the following: 1, 2, 3, 4, 5, 7, 9, 10, 11, 12, 13, 14, 17, 18, 19, 20, 21, 22, 24, 25, 27 and 31. For the frontispiece, which is from Hassell's *Tour of the Grand Junction*, and 15, 16, 26 and 28 I am grateful to the Hugh McKnight Photography collection. 30 and 32 were supplied by Robert Wilson, 6 by Edward Paget Tomlinson and the others are from my own collection. For the other illustrations I am grateful to Robert Wilson who has drawn most of them for me. Many of the maps are based upon the Ordnance Survey maps with the sanction of the Controller of HM Stationery Office—Crown copyright reserved—and the others are based on plans supplied by the British Waterways Board. The Grand Junction committee seal and the tunnel tug ticket are from the Waterways Museum and the share transfer is reproduced with the permission of Bedford County Record Office.

Lock and Distance Table

Main Line	ft	in	Main Line	ft	in
Braunston flight nos 1–6	35	4	Cowroast 46	6	0
			Dudswell Two 47 & 48	13	5
Rise to Braunston			Northchurch Top 49	6	9
summit	35	4	Northchurch 50 (Bush's)	6	10
			Gas Two 51/52 North-		
Long Buckby flight 7–13	62	9	church	13	5
Stoke Bruerne flight 14–			Berkhamsted Top 53	5	10
20	55	10	Sweeps Two 54 & 55	11	1
Cosgrove 21 (Greenbridge)	3	4	Topside 56, Berkhamsted	8	0
			Bottomside 57, Bourne End	8	6
Fall to Fenny Pound	121	11	Sewerage 58, Bourne End	6	1
			Bourne End Bottom 59	6	9
Fenny Stratford 22	1	0	Winkwell Two 60 & 61	13	7
Stoke Hammond 23			Boxmoor Top 62		
(Talbots)	7	5	(Slaughters)	6	8
Soulbury Three 24–26	20	3	Fishery 63, Boxmoor	7	1
Leighton 27 (Town			Boxmoor Bottom 64	7	1
Lock)	6	8	Apsley Top 65	4	7
Grove 28	7	6	Apsley Middle 66	5	3
Church 29	6	10	Apsley Bottom 67	6	3
Slapton 30 (Neal's)	7	1	Nash Mill Two 68 & 69	12	2
Horton 31 (Poole's)	6	9	Kings Langley 69A	8	9
Corketts Two, Ivinghoe			Home Park Mill 70	5	3
32/33	14	3	Home Park Farm 71	6	11
Nagshead Three 34/36	20	4	Hunton Bridge Two 72		
Marsworth Two 37 & 38	14	4	& 73	11	2
Marsworth flight 39–45	42	9	Lady Capel's 74	5	4
			Cassiobury Park Two		
Rise to Tring Summit	155	2	75 & 76	10	0
			Ironbridge 77, Watford	7	4

Main Line	ft	in	Leicester Line	ft	in
Cassiobridge, Watford	9	0	Watford flight 1–7	54	1
Common Moor 79,					
Croxley	9	5	Rise to Twenty Mile		
Lot Mead 80 (Lock 80)	6	3	Summit	54	1
Batchworth 81, Rick-					
mansworth	6	8	Foxton flight 8–17	75	2
Stockers 82	5	2			
Springwell 83	7	11	Fall to Old Union		
Copper Mill 84, Harefield	5	10	Canal	75	2
Black Jack's 85, Harefield	3	8			
Widewater 86, Harefield	8	0	Kibworth flight 18–21	26	10
Denham 87 (Denham			Cranes 22 (Aqueduct)	4	11
Deep)	11	1	Newton Three 23–25	21	5
Uxbridge 88	4	7	Wigston flight 26–29	29	6
Cowley 89	6	5	Kilby Bridge 30	6	2
			Double Rail 31 (Elwell's)	7	6
Fall to the Long Level	294	1	Ervin's 32 (Irving's)	7	1
			Bush 33	7	4
Norwood Two 90 & 91	15	9	Little Glen 34 (Dunn's)	5	10
Hanwell flight 92–97	52	5	Whetstone Lane 35		
Osterley 98	5	6	(Brick Yard)	6	0
Clitheroe's 99, New			Gees 36	7	4
Brentford	7	7	Blue Bank 37	7	9
Brentford Gauging 100	5	4	Kings 38	7	8
			Aylestone Mill 39	4	10
Fall to the river Thames	86	7	St Marys Mill 40	3	2
			New 41, Leicester (Toll-		
Thames 101 (tidal lock)	–	–	house)	7	6
			Fall to the river Soar	160	10

Main Line: 93m 4½f in length. 102 locks admitting craft up to 72ft long and 14¼ft wide. The draught varies considerably up to a maximum of about 4½ft.

Leicester Line: Grand Union section—23m 1f. 17 locks admitting craft 72ft long and 7ft wide. Old Union section—18m 0¾f. 24 locks (originally 25) admitting craft 72ft long and 14ft wide.

Aylesbury Branch: 6m 1½f. 16 locks fall 94ft 8in to Aylesbury. 7ft beam.

Buckingham Branch: 9m 4⅜f. 2 locks rise 13ft 9in to Buckingham. 7ft beam.

Market Harborough Branch: 5m 4⅛f. Level. 14ft beam.

Northampton Branch: 4m 6f. 17 locks fall 107ft 1in to river Nene. 7ft beam.

Old Stratford Branch. 1m 2⅜f. Level. 14ft beam.

Paddington Branch: 13m 4⅜f. Level. 14ft beam.

Rickmansworth Branch: 2⅜f. 1 lock rises 2ft 8in to Rickmansworth. 14ft beam.

Slough Branch. 4m 7⅜f. Level. 14ft beam.

Welford Branch. 1m 5f. 1 lock rises 5ft to Welford. 7ft beam.

Wendover Branch; 6m 6⅛f. Level (stop lock at Tringford). 14ft beam.

Otter Dock, Yiewsley: Main dock & side docks 1m 0⅜f. Level. 14ft beam.

Hanwell Military Depot Loop Line, Southall: 6¾f. Level. 14ft beam.

Weedon Military Dock: 5¼f. Level. 14ft beam. (Government property)

Pocock's Dock, Stockley: 5⅛f.

Willow Tree Dock, Hayes: 4⅞f.

Maypole Dock, Southall: 3½f.

Clayton's Dock, Hayes: 2⅞f.

Passmore's Dock, Southall: 4⅞f.

Troy Branch: 4f. (Private)

Hamborough Dock, Southall: 2⅞f.

Eastwood's Dock, Horton: 2¾f.

APPENDIX 2

Tables of Dividends, Revenue and Tonnages

DIVIDEND TABLE

Year	per cent	Year	per cent	Year	per cent	Year	per cent
1801	2 (a)	1827	13 (b)	1853	4	1879	$4\frac{1}{4}$
1802	—	1828	13	1854	$3\frac{1}{2}$	1880	4
1803	$1\frac{1}{2}$	1829	13	1855	2	1881	4
1804	—	1830	13	1856	$2\frac{3}{4}$	1882	4
1805	1	1831	13	1857	$4\frac{3}{4}$	1883	4
1806	3	1832	12	1858	$3\frac{1}{2}$	1884	4
1807	3	1833	12	1859	$3\frac{3}{4}$	1885	4
1808	4	1834	12	1860	$3\frac{1}{2}$	1886	4
1809	5	1835	12	1861	$3\frac{1}{2}$	1887	4
1810	6	1836	12	1862	4	1888	4
1811	6	1837	12	1863	4	1889	4
1812	7	1838	10	1864	4	1890	4
1813	7	1839	10	1865	4	1891	4
1814	7	1840	8	1866	$4\frac{1}{2}$	1892	4
1815	8	1841	7	1867	$4\frac{1}{4}$	1893	4
1816	2	1842	7	1868	4	1894	4
1817	6	1843	7	1869	$4\frac{1}{4}$	1895	4
1818	$8\frac{1}{2}$	1844	7	1870	4	1896	4
1819	9	1845	7	1871	$3\frac{3}{4}$	1897	4
1820	9	1846	6	1872	4	1898	4
1821	9	1847	5	1873	4	1899	4
1822	10	1848	5	1874	$4\frac{1}{2}$	1900	4
1823	10	1849	5	1875	3	1901	4
1824	11 (b)	1850	4	1876	3	1902	4
1825	13 (b)	1851	3	1877	3	1903	3
1826	13 (b)	1852	$3\frac{1}{2}$	1878	3	1904	3

Year	per cent	Year	per cent	Year	per cent	Year	per cent
1905	3	1911	3	1917	2½	1923	4
1906	3	1912	3	1918	3½	1924	4
1907	3	1913	3 (c)	1919	3¾	1925	4
1908	3	1914	3½	1920	3¾	1926	4
1909	3	1915	3	1921	3¾	1927	4
1910	3	1916	3	1922	3¾	1928	4

Notes:

(a) Initial dividend declared June 1801 and paid February 1803.

(b) Including bonus payment.

(c) Dividends were paid free of income tax up to 1913 but from 1914 tax was deducted.

TONNAGE REVENUE TABLE

Year	£	Year	£	Year	£	Year	£
1795	377	1817	145,558	1839	138,263	1861	68,873
1796	2,120	1818	169,922	1840	121,140	1862	72,702
1797	6,250	1819	157,633	1841	121,753	1863	74,007
1798	8,343	1820	151,525	1842	113,012	1864	75,638
1799	9,973	1821	159,600 (a)	1843	116,686	1865	76,830
1800	17,176	1822	153,620	1844	123,018	1866	74,894
1801	19,699	1823	169,085	1845	106,102	1867	68,422
1802	26,541	1824	178,155	1846	82,044	1868	68,531
1803	22,782	1825	187,532	1847	86,357	1869	63,996
1804	39,409	1826	178,827	1848	79,374	1870	59,741
1805	68,555	1827	189,131	1849	83,748	1871	57,905
1806	87,392	1828	181,932	1850	81,565	1872	62,537
1807	92,602	1829	181,144	1851	79,586	1873	67,601
1808	107,295	1830	176,541	1852	77,814	1874	66,082
1809	127,404	1831	168,540	1853	79,618		
1810	142,979	1832	167,039	1854	82,357		
1811	138,998	1833	170,460	1855	71,679	1923	65,661 (b)
1812	141,911	1834	174,722	1856	73,886	1924	68,070 (b)
1813	168,390	1835	180,125	1857	70,521	1925	68,928 (b)
1814	155,008	1836	198,086	1858	67,365	1926	68,837 (b)
1815	147,857	1837	155,718	1859	67,070	1927	71,062 (b)
1816	127,130	1838	152,657	1860	68,896	1928	71,375 (b)

Notes: (a) estimated; (b) including wharfage receipts.

TONNAGE FIGURES *for some of the more important Traffics* 1904–28

	1904 tons	1910 tons	1916 tons	1922 tons	1928 tons
Ashes & roughdust from Paddington	100,249	77,249	82,969	152,742	163,540
Clay & excavations from Paddington	372,263	114,688	88,275	54,135	49,356
Manure from Paddington	45,669	31,488	17,233	8,277	7,498
Slop & sweepings from Paddington	117,510	80,802	37,711	25,503	25,736
Sand & gravel to Padd'n & Brentford	83,918	50,996	68,872	97,682	108,426
Gravel & ballast south from Denham	130,779	90,009	56,024	130,877	113,936
Sand south from Leighton Buzzard	29,450	31,361	23,465	23,148	29,014
Thames ballast from Brentford	16,630	6,079	117	4,352	2,192
Roadstone from Warwickshire	10,373	9,528	4,606	7,277	6,092
Roadstone from Leicestershire	6,738	2,756	763	668	—
Lime & cement south from Harefield	14,065	19,768	19,812	23,263	30,217
Lime & cement from Stockton	5,309	502	482	137	—
Chalk from Harefield	29,258	11,938	379	5,083	4,790
Bricks north from Cowley district	11,297	15,320	2,220	430	—
Bricks south from Cowley district	104,467	28,223	7,033	2,522	797
Bricks from Gayton & Stoke	12,117	5,097	131	19	—
Grain from Brentford	59,658	54,284	38,020	42,280	45,351
Timber from Brentford	26,720	28,736	15,088	21,587	54,217
Sleepers Brentford to GWR Hayes	20,767	21,532	15,755	14,798	15,679
Sugar from Brentford & Paddington	—	—	23,476	29,073	33,935

Traffic to John Dickinson's Apsley, Croxley and Nash mills

	1904 tons	1910 tons	1916 tons	1922 tons	1928 tons
Paper from the mills	6,286	6,677	9,350	6,957	8,045
Materials from Paddington	4,801	6,695	5,064	4,908	4,592
Raw materials from Brentford	10,479	15,628	12,119	15,603	24,979
Coal to the mills	40,480	43,262	37,025	33,794	45,257

The materials to Dickinson's mills included rags, waste and shavings from Paddington and woodpulp, chemicals, china clay and esparto grass from Brentford.

Gas works traffic in London area

	1904 tons	1910 tons	1916 tons	1922 tons	1928 tons
Coal to Southall	53,703	64,935	32,249	29,034	—
Oil to Southall	5,819	6,695	7,667	4,936	10,744
Coal to Uxbridge	5,704	8,760	10,414	16,251	18,175
Coal Mitre Tip to Kensal Green	19,574	30,137	—	66,813	96,352
Coal Regent's Canal to Kensal Green	84,803	84,841	125,259	103,238	100,343
Oil to Kensal Green	5,474	4,920	3,080	7,828	8,150

The Newport Pagnell Canal

The Grand Junction had rejected the idea of a branch canal to Newport Pagnell as early as 1793, probably because the main canal was to pass fairly close to the town in any case. But the people of Newport were anxious to have the branch and again approached the company in 1802. The Grand Junction still refused to act, mainly because money was very short at the time and there were also problems with the supply of water to the stretch of canal between Fenny Stratford and Wolverton which would have to feed the branch.

Feelings in Newport about the need for a connection with the Grand Junction gradually built up and in January 1813 William Praed convened a meeting in the town[1] at which the merits of constructing either a branch canal or a railway from the main canal at Great Linford were discussed. A committee was set up to pursue the railway proposal but the idea was dropped soon after. At the same time a final request was made to the Grand Junction to build a branch canal, which was turned down yet again. The people of Newport Pagnell then showed considerable initiative in deciding to try and make the connection themselves.[2]

A public meeting was held on 20 August 1813, with the local member of Parliament in the chair, which decided to apply to Parliament for a Bill to construct a branch canal. A subscription list was opened, £7,825 being subscribed immediately. George Cooch, a local lawyer, was appointed clerk and solicitor to the undertaking; he was destined to stay with the concern throughout its existence. From the start the promoters behind this project had their eyes on more ambitious schemes and the committee was told to keep in view the possibility of extending the canal to Olney, Bedford or elsewhere.[3] Indeed at one time the Newport Pagnell Canal in some people's minds was to be merely the first link in a new connection between the Grand Junction and the river Great Ouse, thus forming a major east-west waterways route between the Midlands and East Anglia.

A survey was put in hand by Benjamin Bevan, who estimated

£12,650 would be needed to build the first part of the canal to Newport. His plans were approved at a meeting on 9 November and a call of 2½ per cent was made to meet the expenses. There was little opposition, although the Grand Junction, which had agreed to supply water to the branch free of charge, imposed various conditions to protect its own waterway in times of shortage. The Act[4] received the Royal Assent on 17 June 1814. By it the promoters were incorporated as 'The Company of Proprietors of the Newport Pagnell Canal' with power to raise £13,000 in shares of £100, £50 or £25, with a further £7,000 if necessary. Tonnage rates were fixed at a maximum of 6d (2½p) per ton for manure, 1s 6d (7½p) for coal and coke and 2s 6d (12½p) for all other goods.

At the end of November the company advertised for tenders for carrying out the work, specifying that the canal was to be of the same dimensions and built of similar materials as the Northampton branch then under construction.[5] A contract was awarded in December and the work must have started early in 1815 on the canal, which was to be 1¼ miles in length with seven locks. In May 1816 the Grand Junction gave permission for the junction to be made with its waterway and the works were completed at the end of 1816. It had been hoped to open the canal on 2 December 1816,[6] but this had to be deferred until January 1817[7] and at the same time a wharf was opened at Newport.

Trade was not slow to develop. Coal was always by far the most important traffic, coming mainly from collieries in Derbyshire and Leicestershire, but other traffics handled were stone, manure, bricks, grain, timber, malt, oil cake and salt. For the year ending 31 May 1819 almost 9,900 tons were carried and this rose to a peak of 14,887 tons in 1845 but fell to as low as 5,205 tons in 1850. Coal tonnage was just over 7,200 in 1819. It rose to a peak of over 11,700 tons in 1845 when there was a large traffic into Bedfordshire. This dropped off after the railway from Bletchley to Bedford was opened in November 1846; indeed the coal tonnage slumped to an all time low of just under 3,700 tons in 1850, but it recovered quickly to its former levels. Toll revenue in 1819 was £434, with a further £215 coming in from rents mainly from the company's wharves at Great Linford and Newport Pagnell. Toll income reached a peak of £728 in 1845, but declined in 1846 when the toll on coal was reduced from 1s (5p) to 9d following pressure from the Grand Junction.[8] Income from rents remained fairly constant until the 1850s when it declined somewhat as the company was unable to find tenants so easily. The average dividend paid on the company's capital of £14,230 was £2 14s (£2.70) per cent per annum. In 1845 the dividend was as high as 5½ per cent but in other years, when maintenance costs were heavy, the shareholders received nothing. The figures for the years ending 31 May averaged over three-year periods were as follows:[9]

Years	Tonnage	Tolls £	Rents £	Dividend £
1819–21	10,011	456	207	2.00
1822–4	9,065	425	255	1.66
1825–7	7,574	371	256	2.66
1828–30	8,100	385	243	2.83
1831–3	8,215	388	231	3.00
1834–6	6,556	321	233	2.00
1837–9	9,634	449	234	2.50
1840–2	12,910	614	247	2.16
1843–5	12,451	606	234	4.66
1846–8	12,597	512	214	4.16
1849–51	8,331	381	189	3.08
1852–5	9,782	390	189	2.74
1855–7	10,914	428	180	2.66
1858–60	12,004	464	155	3.00
1861–3	11,022	420	155	2.77
1864 only	10,380	414	155	2.87

From these figures it seems the canal was moderately successful, although the very large profits expected by the shareholders never materialised and the ambitious hopes to extend the canal were never fulfilled.

Right at the end of 1845 there was a proposal for a railway from the London & Birmingham Railway at Wolverton through Newport Pagnell to join the Bletchley to Bedford line near Ridgmont. Apparently Robert Stephenson had suggested that the canal could be taken over and used for part of it, and the canal company offered to sell out for the issued capital of £14,230.[10] In February 1846 a provisional agreement for the railway to buy the canal for £10,000 was reached and in March the canal company petitioned Parliament in support of the railway Bill. But at the end of the month the Grand Junction presented a petition against the scheme and, partly as a result of this, partly because of a general hardening of opinion in Parliament against arrangements between canal and railway companies, the scheme was withdrawn in May 1846.

Towards the end of 1862 another proposal was made, this time for a railway branch from Wolverton to Newport Pagnell, with possible extensions to Olney and Wellingborough, again using the bed of the canal between Great Linford and Newport. The canal company was still keen to sell and asked for £9,000 in December.[11] This was agreed and a formal contract was drawn up between the canal company and the proposed Newport Pagnell Railway Company, which the canal company proprietors approved at a special meeting in April 1863. Once again the Grand Junction strongly opposed the plan, as did various merchants who used the canal, but on 29 June 1863 an Act[12] was passed authorising the canal's closure and the building of the railway. In fact the canal was closed after 8 September 1864, the railway company paying over the £9,000 on 9 September, and a closing down sale was held at Linford wharf on 26 September at which the company sold such equipment as was not included in the sale to the railway. After settling the various winding up expenses there remained £8,730 and this was distributed to the canal company proprietors at the rate of £61 7s (£61.35) for each £100 share.[13] A gratuity of £50 was paid to George Cooch for his work in winding up the affairs of the company and at the final meeting on 24 October 1864 a special vote of thanks was given him for his services of over forty-eight years. Cooch did receive a small salary for his work, which was on a part-time basis, the company's only other employee being Henry Martyn, who had been its toll clerk and lock-keeper for over twenty-five years. He was awarded a gratuity of £10.

The Newport Pagnell Canal used to leave the Grand Junction by the Great Linford road bridge, where there was a wide basin and a transhipment warehouse. The seven locks, all of which fell to Newport Pagnell, were fairly evenly spaced except for three which were in a flight just outside the town. At Newport there was a basin with two arms on which were several wharves and warehouses.

The railway to Newport was duly built and formally opened on 2 September 1867. Although it gave service to Newport it was a financial failure and eventually it was taken over by the London & North Western Railway. The extension to Olney, although authorised by an Act of 1865, was never completed despite the fact that considerable earthworks were carried out along the route.

Index

References to illustrations are printed in *italics*